THE VENEZUELAN REVOLUTION

★THE VENEZUELAN REVOLUTION

100 Questions—100 Answers

Chesa Boudin, Gabriel González, and Wilmer Rumbos

2/2006
For Dale & George
with rage, love & hope —
Chesa B.

Thunder's Mouth Press
New York

THE VENEZUELAN REVOLUTION
100 Questions—100 Answers

Published by
Thunder's Mouth Press
An imprint of Avalon Publishing Group Inc.
245 West 17th Street, 11th Floor
New York, NY 10011

AVALON
publishing group incorporated

Library of Congress Cataloging-in-Publication Data is available.

ISBN: 1-56025-773-3
ISBN 13: 978-1-56025-773-8

9 8 7 6 5 4 3 2 1

Book design by Maria Elias
Printed in the United States of America
Distributed by Publishers Group West

To our fathers and mothers, who brought politics to our lives

CONTENTS

MAP *xiii*

LIST OF ABBREVIATIONS *xv*

INTRODUCTION *xvii*

TIMELINE *xxv*

I. THE POLITICS OF THE BOLIVARIAN REVOLUTION

1) Who is Hugo Chávez? *1*

2) Is Venezuela ruled by a dictatorial regime? *3*

3) How have relations between Venezuela and the United States evolved since Chávez came to power? *5*

4) What is the political ideology underlying the "Bolivarian" revolutionary process? *7*

5) Is the current government communist? *9*

6) What happened to the traditional political parties? *11*

7) What are the most significant structural changes that have occurred since Chávez was first elected? *12*

8) What problems has the revolution failed to resolve? *14*

9) Is this just another military government? *15*

10) Are the changes in Venezuela truly revolutionary? *17*

II. INTERNATIONAL RELATIONS

11) What is the Venezuela-U.S. "battle of microphones"? *19*

12) What are Venezuela's new strategic alliances? *21*

13) Is Venezuela starting a regional arms race? *23*

14) Why is Venezuela opposed to the Free Trade
Area of the Americas (FTAA)? 25

15) Why has there been tension between Venezuela and Colombia? 26

16) Does Chávez's government ally with "terrorist" governments? 28

17) What do people mean when they talk about
an oil foreign policy? 29

18) How does Venezuela prioritize relations with
Latin American countries? 30

19) Why has Venezuela positioned itself as a leader among
developing countries 31

20) What are the primary weaknesses and strengths of Venezuela's
foreign policy? 32

III. THE NEW CONSTITUTION

21) What was the significance of the change from the
Fourth to the Fifth Republic? 35

22) Why did Venezuela write a new constitution? 36

23) What was the legal process for writing and passing the
new constitution? 37

24) Does the new constitution guarantee human rights and
civil rights? 38

25) Is this constitution really innovative? 39

26) How was the new constitution received outside of Venezuela? 41

27) Have the Venezuelan people accepted the new constitution
as their own? 42

28) What were the consequences of the "enabling laws"? 43

29) How did the new constitution change the political
role of the military? 44

30) What kind of government does the new constitution establish? 46

IV. PARTICIPATORY DEMOCRACY

31) What is participatory and "protagonistic" democracy? 49

32) What are the impacts of participatory democracy? 50

33) How have marginalized groups become active in the
political process? 52

34) What is the idea of one big middle class? 53

35) How have women been affected by participatory democracy? 54

36) How has this model of democracy impacted crime, urban security,
and people in Venezuelan jails and prisons? 56

37) How has this model of democracy impacted the
opposition to the Chávez government? 58

38) How has this new model of democracy impacted state-run
corporations? 59

39) How has this model of democracy been received outside of
Venezuela? 61

40) What is innovative about this model of democracy? 62

V. THE MISSIONS AND SOCIAL PROGRAMS

41) What are the missions? 65

42) What are the successes and failures of the Mission Barrio Adentro
("In the Neighborhood")? 66

43) What are the Bolivarian Schools? 67

44) What are the educational missions
(Robinson, Ribas, Sucre, Simoncito . . .)? 69

45) What is Mission Habitat? 70

46) What is Mission Vuelvan Caras? 72

47) What is Mission Mercal? 72

48) What is Mission Guaicaipuro? 74

49) What is Mission Miranda? 75

50) What are the primary failures and successes of the missions? 76

VI. THE APRIL 11, 2002, COUP

51) What happened on April 11 and 12, 2002? 79

52) Why was there a coup? *82*

53) Who was involved in the conspiracy? *83*

54) What was the role of the media? *84*

55) What were the interim government's first steps? *86*

56) Was the United States involved? *87*

57) Why did the coup fail? *89*

58) How was President Chávez rescued? *91*

59) How did the world react to the coup? *92*

60) What was the "constitutional coup"? *93*

VII. THE MEDIA

61) What is happening with the media in Venezuela? *95*

62) Who owns the leading private media? *96*

63) Is it true that the media have "functioned like political parties"? *97*

64) How did the media operate under previous governments? *98*

65) How has the government confronted its problems with the private media? *100*

66) How has this government supported independent media? *101*

67) What are the primary criticisms of Venezuela with regard to freedom of expression and the press? *102*

68) What is the "gag law" or the Social Responsibility in Radio and Television Law? *103*

69) How do international institutions and NGOs present this issue? *105*

70) Is there freedom of speech in Venezuela? *106*

VIII. OIL

71) What are the prospects for the global energy industry? *109*

72) How did PDVSA, a state-owned company, avoid working for the previous Venezuelan governments? *111*

73) What was the December 2002 oil strike? *112*

74) What is "Petroamérica"? *114*

75) Is it true that Venezuela gives free oil to Cuba? *115*

76) What kinds of investments does the Venezuelan government have in the United States? *117*

77) How has Venezuela's oil policy changed under Chávez? *118*

78) How did Venezuela contribute to the launching and the relaunching of OPEC? *119*

79) How does the opposition view the new PDVSA? *120*

80) What is the mandate of the new PDVSA? *121*

IX. ECONOMY AND LAND REFORM

81) What is Venezuela's current economic model? *123*

82) What is the government's international finance policy? *124*

83) What is endogenous development? *126*

84) What is the process for urban land reform? *127*

85) How is agrarian reform being implemented? *129*

86) Does the government respect private property? *131*

87) What is Venezuela's food-security doctrine? *132*

88) What are the primary successes and failures of the new political economy? *133*

89) How have the changes in the economic model affected "average" people? *135*

90) Do the changes amount to an economic revolution? *136*

X. THE FUTURE OF THE BOLIVARIAN REVOLUTION

91) What are the future prospects for President Chávez? *137*

92) Will there be another coup attempt? *138*

93) Will Venezuela's democracy become a dictatorship? *139*

94) What changes can be expected in terms of freedom of speech? *139*

95) Will corruption continue unabated? *140*

96) What are the prospects for the development of
Venezuela's political economy? *141*

97) What are the prospects for Venezuela's oil industry? *142*

98) What are the prospects for the development of the missions? *143*

99) Will Venezuela cut off relations with Colombia and the
United States? *143*

100) What are the future prospects for the Bolivarian Revolution? *145*

NOTES *147*

SUGGESTIONS FOR FURTHER READING *151*

ACKNOWLEDGMENTS *155*

AUTHOR BIOS *156*

LIST OF ABBREVIATIONS

AD: Acción Democrática (Democratic Action). One of the two dominant parties during the Punto Fijo era. Social Democratic.

ALBA: Bolivarian Alternative for the Americas, Chávez's alternative to the FTAA

CIA: Central Intelligence Agency

CNE: National Electoral Council

COPEI: Comité de Organización Política Electoral Independiente (Committee of Independent Electoral Political Organizations). One of the two dominant parties during the Punto Fijo era. Social Christian.

CTV: Confederación de Trabajadores de Venezuela (Confederation of Venezuelan Workers)

CVG: Venezuelan Guayana Corporation

FARC: Fuerzas Armadas Revolucionarias de Colombia

Fedecámaras: Federación de Cámaras y Asociaciones de Comercio y Producción de Venezuela (Federation of Chambers of Commerce and of Production of Venezuela)

FTAA: Free Trade Area of the Americas

GDP: Gross Domestic Product

IMF: International Monetary Fund

MAS: Movimiento Al Socialismo (Movement Toward Socialism Party)

MVR: Movimiento Quinta República (Fifth Republic Movement). The political party founded in 1997 to support Hugo Chávez's presidential candidacy.

NAFTA: North American Free Trade Association

NED: National Endowment for Democracy

OAS: Organization of American States

OPEC: Organization of the Petroleum Exporting Countries

OTI: Office of Transition Initiatives

PCV: Partido Comunista de Venezuela (Venezuelan Communist Party)

PDVSA: Petróleos de Venezuela, Sociedad Anónima (Venezuelan Oil Company Incorporated, Venezuela's state-owned oil company)

PPT: Patria Para Todos (Homeland for All Party)

UBV: Universidad Bolivariana de Venezuela (Bolivarian University of Venezuela)

UNESCO: United Nations Educational, Scientific and Cultural Organization

URD: Unión República Democrática (Democratic Republican Union Party)

USAID: United States Agency for International Development

INTRODUCTION

I stepped out of the hot sun and into the unlit home of José, Rose, and their two young grandchildren. The house was made of tin, cardboard, and the odd scrap of wood. The dirt floor was wet with the swell of groundwater forced up by a nearby dam, and the frame of their shack lurched dangerously to one side. As my eyes adjusted to the darkness, I noticed their walls were covered with pro-Chávez paraphernalia—assorted posters, magnets, and a headband reading *Uh! Ah! Chávez No Se Va!* José and Rose, it turned out, were both *Chavistas*, as people who support President Hugo Chávez and his democratic, peaceful Bolivarian Revolution are known in Venezuela.

Rose invited me to sit down on a makeshift chair and handed me a year-old piece of newspaper. The headline declared that their barrio had been condemned because of dangerous erosion caused by the groundwater that was at that very moment wetting my leather shoes. Their *rancho*, as the shacks and shanties of Venezuela are called, was clearly no place to raise a family, but it turned out that the entire area had been deemed unsuitable for human habitation. I couldn't help asking myself why, a year after the *rancho* they called home had been publicly condemned, they would still enthusiastically support their government.

• • •

Venezuela, roughly twice the size of California, is the northernmost country in South America, and has nearly two thousand miles of Caribbean coast. In addition to its stellar beaches and dozens of small islands, Venezuela boasts

Angel Falls—the world's highest waterfall at over three thousand feet—
Andean peaks reaching over sixteen thousand feet, virgin Amazon rain
forest, and the Orinoco River, whose delta is roughly the size of Belgium.
Venezuela's twenty-five million people, 20 percent of whom live in the
Caracas metropolitan area, are a mix of European, Indian, and African
descent. Venezuela's subsoil happens to hold arguably the world's largest
energy reserves, made up of petroleum and natural gas. It is this fact, more
than anything else, that has made internal political developments in
Venezuela since 1998 a cause for international concern. In that year, Hugo
Chávez was elected president on an independent ticket calling for democratic "revolution." Only in the context of the country's recent history is it
possible to understand why a decisive majority of Venezuelans would vote for
a self-proclaimed revolutionary.

Beginning with Spanish colonization in the 1500s, a series of dictatorial
regimes ruled Venezuela until 1958, when a power-sharing agreement between
leading political parties led to the creation of what became essentially a two-
party democracy. Politicians from the Acción Democrática (AD) and Comité
de Organización Política Electoral Independiente (COPEI) parties would
share power for the next forty years, even as their policies led the country into
a protracted national crisis.

Oil prices dropped in the 1980s, leaving Venezuela unable to pay its
recently acquired foreign debt: the country suffered harshly during a decade-
long regional economic recession. Inflation accelerated, and in 1983, a massive bank failure combined with widespread embezzlement and capital flight
wiped out the savings of much of the middle class. In the midst of this recession, marked by spiraling national debt, international financial institutions
promoted neoliberal economic policies that became a central part of the
Venezuelan government program for over a decade. These market-liberalization
policies—based on reducing import taxes and tariffs, cutting public spending
and social services, privatizing national industries, and encouraging foreign
investment—were pushed on consecutive Venezuelan governments as the
only way to modernize and develop the country. In Venezuela as elsewhere,
structural adjustment packages required a massive sacrifice on the part of
the majority of the people—though they tended to benefit local and international economic elites—as the government devalued the currency, cut back
on services and labor protections, and began to privatize state assets.

The leaders of the AD and COPEI parties were the ones implementing these policies year after year, and the popular response became explosive. In February 1989, in the wake of the imposition of yet another round of neoliberal policies, people took to the streets by the hundreds of thousands to protest in what became known as the "*Caracazo.*" The military was called in, and the protests were put down with a hail of bullets. Some 5,000 smaller protests would follow over the next three years—an average of 4.5 protests per day. The failure of politicians to take responsibility for, or to represent the interests of, the masses led to an antiparty reaction throughout the country, and to two failed coup attempts—one of which was led by the then Lieutenant Colonel Hugo Chávez.

The political crisis was exacerbated by a continuing economic decline that disproportionately affected the poor majority of the country. In 1989 alone the poverty rate increased from 46 to 62 percent of the population, while the number of those living in extreme poverty more than doubled, up to 30 percent. Meanwhile, the government sharply reduced funding for everything from education to health care, from housing to rural development. Inflation climbed above 100 percent in 1996. By 1997, the wealthiest 5 percent of the country had incomes that were 53.1 times greater than the poorest 5 percent; roughly 85 percent of the country lived in poverty and 67 percent lived in extreme poverty, earning less than $2 per day. More than three-quarters of the farmland was owned by just 3 percent of the population. Over half of the workforce was in the informal economy. Venezuelans had come to view their political parties and system as unrepresentative and unredeemable. The majority gave up on institutional reform, demanding revolutionary change instead.

The credibility crisis for the entire system of government—and particularly for the ruling parties—set the stage for the rise of new political actors and organizations. Hugo Chávez and the Fifth Republic Movement (MVR) filled that void and answered the people's call for peaceful revolutionary change. Although the unraveling of the country's representative democracy might have led to widespread disillusionment with democracy itself, in this case the opposite has proven true; Chávez has presided over a dramatic upsurge in support for democracy in Venezuela, bucking the regional trend.

Latinobarómetro, a Chilean polling company, carries out annual surveys in every Latin American country; pollsters ask people if democracy is preferable to any other kind of government and have returned remarkable results. From 1996 to 2004, support for democracy decreased by 8 percent on average throughout the region, while in some countries—such as Nicaragua and Paraguay—it decreased by as much as 20 percent; people are disillusioned with the way democracy has been imposed on them. Meanwhile, support for democracy in Venezuela increased by 12 percent—more than any other country in the region—up to 74 percent of the population, as compared to the regional average of 53 percent. Something unique and exciting is happening in Venezuela.

A few days after Latinobarómetro's results were published, on August 15, 2004, President Chávez shocked the world by decisively winning a recall referendum that the opposition to his revolutionary government had initiated to drive him from office. It was the most recent in a series of attempts the old political elite had made to reclaim power, including a short-lived coup d'état in 2002 and several devastating national strikes. With every failure of the opposition to reclaim their traditional control of government, Chávez seemed to grow stronger. He deepened and extended his revolutionary program—forcing the state oil company to fund a massive social-welfare initiative known as the "missions," beginning a progressive agrarian-reform process, and consolidating control over state power through democratic victories and institutional reforms. The traditional economic and political elites in Venezuela cried foul, and warned the world of Chávez's authoritarian tendencies, attacks on freedom of speech, and the "Cubanization of Venezuela."

It was in this context that I decided to travel to Venezuela to see for myself. Was Chávez just another military demagogue dressed up in democratic coattails who, once elected, immediately began consolidating personal power and cracking down on civil liberties and the political opposition? Or was he someone who gained power through fair and free elections and who, once elected, immediately launched an ambitious plan to correct decades of inequities and injustice by harnessing the country's vast oil resources in the interest of the poor and dispossessed, thereby presenting the continent and the world with an alternative to U.S. hegemony?

When I got to Caracas in November 2004, I realized how much more complicated it all was. I had endless questions for every Venezuelan—from taxi drivers to university professors, from peasant farmers to presidential advisors—who would put up with my ignorance and naiveté.

One particularly well-informed and patient friend suggested, half joking, that with all the questions I had we should make a book out of them for other people from the United States who were interested in learning about the

Venezuelan democratic revolution but did not have the luxury of moving to Caracas to investigate for themselves. I took him too seriously and, with the support of a mutual Venezuelan friend, the three of us embarked on this project.

This book attempts to provide an easy-to-read introduction to the dramatic changes under way in Venezuela. Our approach was not academic. Since questions tend to be thematic rather than chronological, so too is this book. Though we have chosen the order of chapters and questions for specific reasons, the book need not be read straight from beginning to end. Because *The Venezuelan Revolution* covers a wide range of topics, it does not go into great depth on any one. Providing as much background information as possible in a short space, every chapter, we hope, reveals the immense complexity of the issues that lie beneath the surface. We also hope it will inspire further study.

The process of writing a book for readers in the United States with two Venezuelan coauthors presented constant challenges. I was acutely aware of the ways in which the Venezuelan revolution has been portrayed in the United States and in English-language media, while my coauthors refused to allow the opposition's framework to define the book. I was an outsider peering in, while they were insiders reaching out. I brought the perspective of a historian, while Gabriel and Wilmer brought those of a political analyst and a journalist, respectively. Both of my coauthors' experiences over the last seven years have led them, like so many millions of Venezuelans, to support the Chávez government, while I was skeptical. We did all of the writing and editing in Spanish, and I alone rewrote the entire book in English.

Translation is imprecise at best, and in most cases I opted to rewrite instead of translate as such. Yet even with the many answers that I had written in Spanish myself, I encountered problems that ran deeper than linguistics as I rewrote in English: many words or phrases have a unique cultural-political meaning in Venezuela that is lost even when using the most precise English equivalent. For example, people at all levels of society and all along the political spectrum in Venezuela call the complex range of political and economic interests that oppose the Bolivarian Revolution "the opposition." The opposition is a fluid coalition of people, groups, and factions, and labeling these complex interests simply "the opposition" feels reductionist in English. Yet, in Venezuela's context of political polarization, of extremes, and of high-stakes political maneuvering, this shorthand is universally used and understood. When writing in English, I have tried to be as loyal as possible to the Venezuelan linguistic framework so as to convey the political-cultural context.

In the process of researching, writing, and living in Venezuela, I became convinced that, for all of its problems—and there are many—the Chávez government is both profoundly democratic and committed to working for the poor masses. Chávez and the decisive majority of Venezuelans that elected him have the right to steer their own course, to make their own mistakes, to find their own solutions, and to invent their own model, without the interference of foreign governments or violent coups.

I also came to believe that we in the United States have much to learn from Venezuela's current political process, which emerged because of the failures of a deeply entrenched, exclusionary two-party system with remarkable parallels to our own. For how long has our government failed to represent the working majority in our country? Why do we allow our unparalleled resources to be so heavily invested in weapons of mass destruction and war? People throughout the world, including those in Venezuela, see our government as interventionist, imperialist, and—simply put—bullying. Venezuela's Simón Bolívar, leader of the armies that drove colonial Spain from the northern half of South America in the early 1800s, is an eternal and omnipresent hero throughout Latin America. On his deathbed in 1829, Bolívar wrote that "the United States seems destined by providence to plague America with misery in the name of liberty." Today, far too many Latin Americans identify those words as prescient.

Those of us from the United States who don't want our government to continue proving Bolívar's predictions right have an obligation to do more than just vote. In the 2004 presidential election, I, and countless others, had to choose between two candidates who supported war, U.S. foreign intervention, and a wide range of other alienating policies. I arrived in South America frustrated, jaded, and disillusioned. The Venezuelans I met understood—they, too, had spent decades under a two-party democracy that continually failed the majority. Through their words and deeds, Venezuelans are sharing with me an exciting alternative and participatory model for democracy that has attracted the attention of people all over the world.

• • •

As José was showing me his prized possession—a sewing machine—and a few hats he stitched and sold to make a living, I asked him why he supported Chávez so enthusiastically—the kind of question that had brought me to Venezuela in the first place. He put down the stack of multicolored cotton caps and said, "At first we voted for Chávez because he wasn't from AD or COPEI. We keep voting for him because he is making a difference in our day-to-day life. When Chávez founded Mission Robinson, he gave me the opportunity to learn to read—I could not help my children with their studies, but now I help my grandchildren. Chávez sent doctors to live and work in our barrio, and he makes sure we can afford to pay for our food. We have a long way to go, but Chávez gives us the hope to keep fighting."

José and Rose lived in the barrio known as Alianza on the outskirts of San Cristóbal, Táchira State, but I could have been in any one of the country's countless barrios and they could have been any one of the millions of families living below the poverty line in oil-rich Venezuela. Today, Venezuela is in the midst of a fascinating and immensely complex peaceful, democratic revolution. This book is but a small window into that world; it is no substitute for walking through the barrios above Caracas, for partaking in conversations with the country's elite in the Sambil mall, for visiting the patients in Mission Barrio Adentro, or for letting the people of Venezuela speak for themselves.

Chesa Boudin
Caracas, July 2005

Timeline

1498   Christopher Columbus lands on Venezuela's coast and two years later Spain begins colonizing the area.

1821   Spain recognizes Venezuela's independence after *El Libertador* Simón Bolívar wins a decisive military victory against the royalists.

1958   Venezuela's representative democracy is founded in the Punto Fijo power-sharing agreement between the AD and COPEI parties, who will alternate control of the government for the next forty years.

1976   The petroleum and iron industries are nationalized.

1983   The government stops propping up the national currency, resulting in "Black Friday" and a national financial crisis.

1989   On February 16, two weeks after taking office, President Carlos Andrés Pérez announces a series of "neoliberal" structural adjustment policies recommended by the IMF, including a sharp rise in gas prices, a decrease in public services, and the elimination of social subsidies.

1989   On February 27 and 28, massive protests against the neoliberal policies shut down Caracas. The military is called in to restore order, leading to several thousand civilian deaths. There are an average of 4.5 protests per day for the next three years.

1992   On February 4, then Lieutenant Colonel Hugo Chávez leads an unsuccessful military coup attempt. Chávez takes responsibility in a national television address and becomes a national hero—but is sent to jail.

1992   On November 27, a second military coup attempt also fails.

1993   President Carlos Andrés Pérez is impeached.

1994   Hugo Chávez is pardoned and released under newly elected president Rafael Caldera.

1998   Chávez is elected president of Venezuela with 62 percent of the vote.

1999   Chávez takes office and immediately calls for a referendum to convoke a constitutional assembly.

1999   On December 15, the new constitution comes into effect.

2000   Venezuela is named secretary general of OPEC, a position Saudi Arabia had held for the previous twenty-seven years.

2001   President Chávez decrees the forty-nine enabling laws, including the so-called Land Law, Hydrocarbons Law, and Microfinance Law. These laws radicalize the opposition.

2002   On April 11, massive protests against the Chávez government set up a coup attempt led by Pedro Carmona Estanga, president of the Venezuelan Chamber of Commerce (Fedecámaras). The coup plot is supported by dozens of generals in the armed forces and facilitated by the private media. Carmona dissolves the National Assembly and the Supreme Court, and empowers himself to remove any elected official in the country from office.

2002   On April 14, President Chávez returns to power thanks to widespread popular protests and the unity between the loyal members of the military and the people in the streets.

2002–03 In December a national strike is called to undermine President Chávez's government. The strike lasts sixty-two days and causes billions of dollars in damage to oil wells and refineries. Workers loyal to Chávez retake control of the national oil industry installations and Chávez fires some nineteen thousand members of PDVSA's management and staff who had supported the strike and converts one of their office buildings into the new free Bolivarian University of Venezuela (UBV).

2003   The social programs known as the missions are founded. These programs include free primary health care, a literacy campaign, soup kitchens, and more.

2004   On August 15, President Chávez wins a recall referendum with 59 percent of the vote. The referendum was an opposition attempt to remove him from power before the end of his term.

2004   In October, in the regional elections, the pro-Chávez coalition wins 274 of Venezuela's 334 mayoralities (210 of them within Chávez's MVR party), and pro-Chávez candidates win 20 of the 22 state governorships.

2005   In May polls show popular support for Chávez at an all-time high of 70.5 percent.

The Politics of the Bolivarian Revolution

(1) Who is Hugo Chávez?

President Hugo Rafael Chávez Frías was born in 1954 in a rural town called Sabaneta in Barinas State. Both his mother and father were schoolteachers and they raised their large family in humble circumstances. While his parents worked in small out-of-the-way towns and villages, Chávez's grandmother, Rosines, raised him.

Chávez turned seventeen with the dream of becoming a professional baseball player, and he enrolled in the military academy, hoping it would launch his career as a big-league pitcher. The baseball career never worked out, but Chávez did graduate as an officer in the Venezuelan military and go on to do postgraduate work in political science at Simón Bolívar University.

On February 27, 1989, President Carlos Andrés Pérez ordered the army to fire on unarmed civilians protesting his economic policies, in what became known as the *Caracazo*. The order led to the deaths of thousands of civilians, though the exact numbers and circumstances are still disputed. In the years that followed, there were an average of 4.5 protests per day across Venezuela, and in 1992 Chávez answered the call of these protests by leading an unsuccessful coup attempt.

Then Lieutenant-Colonel Chávez, just thirty-seven years old, became nationally known when, in a brief, seventy-four-second television appearance in the wake of the failed coup, he said: "Comrades, the objectives we set for ourselves have not been possible to achieve for now—"*por ahora*"—but new possibilities will arise again, and the country will be able to move forward to a better future. . . . I alone take responsibility for this Bolivarian military uprising." He encouraged his comrades to give themselves up to avoid further bloodshed. He then spent two years in prison before being released due to national political pressure and the impeachment of President Pérez. After his release, he began organizing throughout the country and decided to run for president in the 1998 electoral cycle. The fact that he had taken responsibility for the failed coup, and his use of the words "*por ahora*," made him a national hero.

Since that victory, President Chávez has become by far the most powerful political figure in Venezuela. Every Sunday, millions of Venezuelans watch and listen as President Chávez talks about politics, history, family, sports, economy, and culture on his TV/radio show *Aló Presidente*. The program usually lasts around five hours, during which he has special guests and accepts call-ins from citizens around the country.

President Chávez accepts notes from people wherever he goes, he enters into the midst of swelling crowds, he speaks at all kinds of public events, and he comes from a working-class background. He does not use scripted speeches for his average of forty hours per week of public speaking.

Chávez's personality, ideas, and actions have aroused both deep sympathy and profound controversy as the country becomes more and more politicized. He presents himself as a champion of the poor, and is widely accepted as such by the poor. His skills as an orator and a political strategist have earned popular support for the peaceful Bolivarian Revolution in spite of the ongoing attacks from the political opposition, who accuse him of being a demagogue with authoritarian tendencies. As the well-known Venezuelan psychiatrist Edmundo Chirinos has put it, "We can know him in depth only if we join the criticism of his adversaries with the idolatry of his followers and strain them through the colander of logic and objectivity."[1]

After six years as head of state, his public approval rating reached 70.5 percent according to a poll released in May 2005 by Datanalysis, a company that has openly declared its opposition to the Chávez government.[2]

(2) Is Venezuela ruled by a dictatorial regime?

Since President Chávez was elected, significant groups within the national and international opposition have claimed that Venezuela no longer has a democratic government. Even before Chávez won the 1998 presidential elections, the media, opposing political parties, cultural and social elites, and the church all expressed their fear that if he were to win the election, Venezuela would quickly transform from a democracy into a dictatorship. They argued that Chávez had all the markings of a dictator in the making, including his military background and his leading participation in the failed 1992 coup d'état. That 1992 coup attempt was neither the first nor the last in Venezuela's tumultuous political history.

Venezuela spent more than half of the twentieth century under the rule of dictatorial regimes—those of Juan Vicente Gómez (1908–1935) and Marcos Pérez Jiménez (1948–1958) lasted the longest. This political legacy, very much present in the living memory of millions of Venezuelans, makes the idea of a dictator all the more real and ominous, contributing to heightened fears of anything that might threaten the continuation of formal democratic rule. Chávez's political adversaries have continually manipulated these fears, especially through their ownership and control of print, TV, and radio news—despite the fact that he came to power and has stayed in power through democratic national elections. Chávez's victory in the 1998 election broke the monopoly of Venezuela's two-party system. He successfully ran against the two dominant political parties, AD and COPEI, which had shared power since the end of Venezuela's last dictatorship in 1958 but which had become increasingly delegitimized throughout the 1980s and 1990s.[3]

Since 1998, President Chávez's government has won nine electoral contests. According to the National Electoral Council (CNE), responsible for organizing and holding all government elections in the country, Chávez won the multicandidate presidential election in December 1998 with 62 percent of the vote; his closest competitor had just 31 percent.[4] In April 1999, a national referendum was called to determine whether or not the country would convene a constitutional assembly—as Chávez proposed—and over 71 percent of the voters supported the proposal. Then, in July 1999, in the elections for delegates to the constitutional assembly, the coalition of parties that President Chávez supported—known as the Patriotic Pole—won

125 of the 131 seats. The next national referendum was held in December 1999 to approve or reject the newly drafted Bolivarian Constitution, and nearly 88 percent of voters approved it. Once the new constitution was in place, all public officials had to be reelected under the new legal code in what were known as the "megaelections" of July 2000; Chávez's presidency was reconfirmed with just shy of 60 percent of the vote. In December, the coalition of parties supporting Chávez won the majority of seats in municipal and gubernatorial elections, though these results are less clear-cut because in many municipalities there were multiple pro-Chávez candidates competing against each other.

Chávez's supporters claim victory in a series of labor union elections from August to October 2000, including 276 unions and 75 labor federations, but the results are unclear. Carlos Ortega, representing the opposition's coalition, and Aristóbulo Istúriz on the pro-Chávez ticket, ran for the presidency of the Confederation of Venezuelan Workers (CTV), then the largest national labor federation and traditionally linked to the AD party. Before the votes could be counted, the opposition cadres commandeered the ballot boxes and declared Ortega the winner. The ballot boxes have yet to be found, and Ortega went on to play a leading role in both the April 2002 coup (discussed in chapter VI) and the December 2002 oil strike (see question 73).

In August 2004, in the wake of a massive opposition signature drive and under international pressure, Chávez submitted himself to a presidential recall referendum and was ratified by over 59 percent of the vote. Finally, in the regional elections held in October 2004, the pro-Chávez coalition won 82 percent (274) of Venezuela's 334 mayoralities (210 of them within Chávez's MVR party), and pro-Chávez candidates won 20 of the 22 state governorships (91 percent).

In the face of this overwhelming record, not only of democratic elections, but also of decisive margins of voter support, spokespeople for the U.S. government and members of Venezuela's opposition, forced to recognize President Chávez's success in the polls, now argue that he is a democratically elected president who governs "undemocratically." The claim that Chávez has "authoritarian tendencies" continues unabated. But his three separate victories in national presidential electoral contests, and his other electoral victories, each in accordance with Venezuela's constitution, discredit the opposition's claims of a Chávez dictatorship.

(3) **How have relations between Venezuela and the United States evolved since Chávez came to power?**

Until President Chávez's election in 1998, the United States was one of Venezuela's closest allies. President Chávez, however, has never had a particularly good relationship with the U.S. government. In 1998, when he was a presidential candidate, the U.S. government denied Chávez a visa on the grounds that he had participated in the 1992 coup. Ironically, on May 31, 2005, President Bush decided to not only grant a visa to but also to have a private meeting with María Corina Machado, who is awaiting trial for treason against Venezuela. Machado participated in the 2002 coup against the Chávez government and was present when Pedro Carmona swore himself in as president and issued his decree dissolving the National Assembly and the Supreme Court, and empowering himself to remove any elected official in the country (discussed in chapter VI). The Bush administration has been unwilling to meet bilaterally with any representatives of the Chávez government, but decided to grant a high-profile meeting to this representative of "Venezuelan civil society." Machado is the director of the Venezuelan nongovernmental organization (NGO) Súmate (Join Up), which was founded to organize support for the recall referendum against Chávez, and which receives a significant portion of its funding from the U.S. government via the National Endowment for Democracy (NED). Bush's decision to meet with Machado is a clear indication of the nature of the relationship between Venezuela and the United States.

As soon as Chávez was elected president, the United States immediately authorized a visa for him to enter the country. Since then Chávez has visited the United States on eight separate occasions. On June 9, 1999, shortly after taking office, he visited both New York and Houston to strengthen ties with international investors and representatives of the oil industry. During his day in New York, he visited the Stock Exchange and the Council on Foreign Relations; he also threw out the first pitch at a Mets game in Shea Stadium. When he passed through Houston, he met the Bush family, including former President George H. W. Bush and then presidential candidate Governor George W. Bush.[5] Despite these visits, President Chávez has never been officially received by an acting president of the United States (Clinton did unofficially receive him), and Venezuelan-U.S. relations have steadily deteriorated.

When President Chávez first took office, his anti-imperialist rhetoric did not seem to bother the Clinton administration, which preferred to wait and see concrete developments instead of reacting to the rhetoric. When the Venezuelan government took a leadership role in the Organization of the Petroleum Exporting Countries (OPEC), cultivated diplomatic relations with Cuba, and openly sought new, nontraditional alliances, the United States reacted negatively. Moreover, President Chávez continually criticizes the U.S. government for such things as its pushing of the Free Trade Area of the Americas (FTAA) and even more so with regard to the invasion and occupation of Afghanistan and Iraq. Likewise, the Venezuelan government has, on countless occasions, accused the U.S. government of intervening in domestic Venezuelan affairs, using Central Intelligence Agency (CIA) documents and NED funding for oppositional NGOs as its primary evidence. Because of these fears of U.S. intervention, in April 2005, when a U.S. military officer was caught taking photos of Venezuelan military installations, Chávez unilaterally terminated a long-standing U.S.-Venezuela military-exchange program.

The U.S. State Department has also openly declared its continued support for the Venezuelan opposition and defines Chávez as a "negative force in the region." While everyone knows that Chávez is attempting to reduce U.S. influence in his country and beyond, he continues to insist that he does not want confrontation, but rather cordial relations, selective cooperation, and mutual respect.

The two countries continue to be interdependent. The United States depends on Venezuela for approximately 12 percent of its daily oil imports (or just over 6 percent of its daily oil consumption), and Venezuela sells roughly 70 percent of its daily oil exports to U.S. markets. The United States consumes 50 percent of all Venezuelan exports, while 35 percent of Venezuelan imports come from U.S. ports, making Venezuela the United States' third most important trading partner in Latin America after Mexico and Brazil. If it were not for this strong economic interdependency, it is possible that economic relations would already have been cut off. At the beginning of 2005, rumors began circulating in the press about Venezuela's interest in selling Citgo, the U.S.-based oil refinery and filling station chain wholly owned by Petróleos de Venezuela, Sociedad Anónima (PDVSA), the Venezuelan state-owned oil company. Rumors and developments such as these have led many lawmakers in Washington to express their fear of the possibility of losing Venezuela's reliable oil supply.

Bilateral relations reached a new low thanks to a series of international developments both in and out of Venezuela. Venezuela's efforts to negotiate a series of light arms purchases from Russia, Brazil, and Spain led to open protest from the White House, the State Department, and the Pentagon (see question 13). Venezuelan government accusations of a U.S. plot to assassinate President Chávez made relations even worse. Finally, in May 2005, Luis Posada Carriles, an admitted anti-Castro terrorist with Venezuelan citizenship, illegally entered the United States from Mexico and requested asylum. Venezuela has had an international arrest warrant pending since he escaped from a Venezuelan jail in 1985 while awaiting trial for the bombing of a Cuban airplane that resulted in seventy-three deaths. The United States has been slow to honor the terms of its 1922 extradition treaty with Venezuela. Instead of extraditing him or trying him as an international terrorist, the United States is holding Posada Carriles on immigration violation charges. On May 22, 2005, President Chávez threatened to cut off diplomatic relations if the United States did not honor its treaty obligations and cooperate in bringing this renowned international terrorist to justice. As this book went to print, the U.S. government was still holding Posada Carriles on immigration charges and had not formally responded to the Venezuelan extradition request.

(4) What is the political ideology underlying the "Bolivarian" revolutionary process?

The ideological roots of the Bolivarian Revolution can be traced to a diverse range of intellectual sources, though the core of the political ideology comes from within the wealth of Venezuela's own cultural history. Bolivarian political ideology derives directly from the works of three long-dead Venezuelans: Simón Bolívar, Simón Rodríguez, and Ezequiel Zamora. Chávez christened the contemporary, ongoing democratic revolution "Bolivarian" in honor of Bolívar (1783–1830), a renowned military strategist and intellectual known in Venezuela as *El Libertador*. Bolívar's military prowess brought him to the leadership of the South American liberation movement against Spanish colonial rule. Armies under his command liberated territory including present-day Venezuela, Colombia, Peru, Ecuador, and Bolivia (named after him, of course). The enormous legacy of his writings covers a range of topics including politics, economics, jurisprudence, education, morality, and civil duty: he was a Renaissance man. Among other things, his works focus on the value of national sovereignty and continental unity, and the construction of strong nations capable of steady development in the midst of adverse circumstances. In Bolívar's last years, his life's project of "La Gran Colombia"—the unified country he tried to form out of Ecuador, Colombia, and Venezuela, and in which he hoped other newly liberated South American nations would join—unraveled before his eyes as the regional oligarchies refused to work together toward his vision.

Simón Rodríguez, another one of the intellectual foundations of today's Bolivarian Revolution, was Simón Bolívar's most influential tutor; the older man instilled in Bolívar a commitment to the concept of liberty. Rodríguez dedicated the bulk of his works to education, which he viewed as necessary since only an educated, conscious populace could construct a free society. As he put it, "To build republics, it is necessary to train republicans." He was acutely aware of the importance, within the newly liberated republics in the region, of developing a system based on local resources and needs. With this in mind he was known to say, "Either we innovate or we deteriorate" (*O inventamos o erramos*).

Ezequiel Zamora was a leader in the Venezuelan Federal War of 1859 who was known for his slogan "Free land and free men." A man of action, he followed in the footsteps of *El Libertador* and sided with the poor and dispossessed against the powerful ruling classes who usurped the independence movement for their own interests. Today's peasant land reform movements in Venezuela carry on his legacy. Together, Bolívar, Rodríguez, and Zamora form the triad that has become known as the "tree with three roots."

The work of these three thinkers was formative for Hugo Chávez, but he also draws on a diverse range of historical figures—including Mahatma Gandhi, Martin Luther King Jr., Jesus Christ, Che Guevara, Karl Marx, José Martí, and countless indigenous leaders from Venezuelan history and that of Latin America as a whole. Chávez defines himself as a Christian, an anti-imperialist, a nationalist, and a leftist.

President Chávez created a nationalist model of endogenous development, or development from within (see question 83) and defense of national sovereignty within Venezuela while working internationally toward an independent foreign policy based on enabling equitable global development and empowering poor countries to face their primary enemy: poverty. To meet these goals, President Chávez argues it is necessary to have a multipolar rather than unipolar system of world power, an argument that often pits him against the U.S. government.

(5) Is the current government communist?

Although the Venezuelan Communist Party (PCV) supports the Chávez government and was the first political party (besides his MVR party) to endorse his presidential candidacy in 1998, its members do not currently have any significant positions in the central government. None of the ministers, members of the National Assembly, state governors, or any other high-ranking public officials are communists.

Nonetheless, some sectors of the opposition in Venezuela denounce the Chávez government as communist. Domestically, this rhetoric serves to scare the people, particularly the middle classes, who fear that their political power and modest economic gains will be lost. Internationally, the rhetoric plays on long-standing fears of communism in the Western Hemisphere that have survived the end of the Cold War. The Venezuelan opposition has, in this sense, worked to encourage the U.S. government to view the Venezuelan government as undemocratic, dictatorial, and generally hostile to U.S. interests. Of course, President Chávez's sharp criticism of U.S. policy—characterized as anti-American—has made that an easy job for the opposition (see question 11). More than his rhetoric, President Chávez's relationships with governments that declare themselves to be communist—such as Cuba and China—have been used in attempts to isolate him domestically and internationally. The portrayal of Venezuela as communist dramatically increased once Cuba began sending thousands of doctors to Venezuela as part of a public health program called Mission Barrio Adentro (see question 42).

The Marxist-Leninist party, Bandera Roja, and the labor party, La Causa Radical, are part of the political opposition and criticize the government for being "neoliberal." These parties argue that the government plans to privatize key state enterprises and that by playing along with an unjust system of international debt financing, it is going to end up handing over all of the country's resources to transnational capitalist interests.

This is just a hint of the complexity of the Venezuelan political scene, in the midst of which President Chávez has put forward the idea for twenty-first-century socialism. He has declared himself to be anticapitalist, arguing for peoples' solidarity over commercial and financial solidarity. In his public speeches, with increasing frequency and sometimes with scathing rhetoric, Chávez has scorned capitalism and embraced the language of socialism.

At the opening ceremony for the Fourth Summit on the Social Debt and Social Charter of the Americas held in Caracas on February 25, 2005, President Chávez solidified what has been a gradual process of change in his discourse with regard to his economic vision. In the early years of his presidency, he had talked about a "third way," a "humanized capitalism." In his remarks at this summit, in an auditorium filled with left-wing delegates, he declared: "The capitalist model makes it impossible to eradicate poverty, inequality. Now, a lot of people have talked and written extensively about a third way, capitalism with a human face . . . trying to put a mask on the monster, but a mask on such a monster will fall apart in the face of reality." In this speech, President Chávez definitively marked a shift toward a socialist vision for Venezuela: "So if capitalism is not the way, then what is? I have no doubt that it is socialism. Now, what is socialism, which version of so many theories? It is safe to say that despite all of the historical experience, all of the achievements and advancements in cases where socialism has been implemented, we will have to invent our own socialism, and that is why these debates, the battle of ideas, is so important; we must invent twenty-first-century socialism. . . ."

Although Chávez has continued to publicly explore his commitment to socialism in most of his appearances, as of June 2005, he had yet to concretely define what it means in practice. In other words, Chávez has put forward the idea of twenty-first-century socialism as an alternative to capitalism, but it's an alternative that has yet to be fully developed or articulated. He suggests that Venezuela must construct its own socialist model rather than following any other country's example. According to him, each country must find its own path, and Venezuela has no interest either in importing a ready-made model or in exporting its budding form of "socialism." While he may not have figured out exactly what the socialism of the twenty-first century is yet, he has some ideas under way, such as endogenous development (see question 83), participatory democracy (discussed in chapter IV), land reform (see question 85), and comanagement (see question 38). A nationwide poll carried out by Seijas & Asociados in late May and early June 2005 showed that about 48 percent of respondents preferred a socialist over a capitalist system, with less than 26 percent preferring the latter. These results, Chávez's rhetoric and the abovementioned initiatives notwithstanding, Venezuela's constitution still protects private property rights, the government still courts international investors, and capitalism is alive and well throughout Venezuela.

(6) What happened to the traditional political parties?

In 1958, the three strongest Venezuelan political parties signed what is known as the Punto Fijo agreement, which established the rules of the game in Venezuela's newfound democratic system. According to the agreement, these parties would share the power, dividing up the government-appointed positions no matter which party won the most votes. The three parties were AD, COPEI, and URD (which fell apart soon after the agreement). And thus the period known as *puntofijism* was born, in which AD and COPEI traded off control of the presidency and the government regularly.

Widespread corruption, clientelism, political demoralization, and the disillusionment of the masses became the hallmarks of both parties' rule. In the presidential elections, these two parties fought for power, leaving the country's smaller, left-of-center parties a distant third. Accusations of electoral fraud were common.

Until Hugo Chávez's entry into the elections of 1998, the Venezuelan political scene had remained relatively uniform. The political elites conspired to keep the Left out of power by controlling elections.

The implosion of the AD and COPEI political parties in 1998 can be attributed to the long-term collapse of a political, economic, and social model that had failed the majority of Venezuelans, who continued to live in extreme poverty—by 1997, 85 percent of the country lived in poverty. As a candidate in 1998, Chávez was new to the political scene and organized around a vision of a different kind of government. His ideas were widely debated in the media and around the country, and he successfully unified a wide range of small, left-wing political parties into what was called the "Patriotic Pole." Chávez's newly formed MVR, along with the new Patria Para Todos (Homeland for All Party, PPT) and the older Movimiento Al Socialismo (Movement Toward Socialism Party, MAS) and PCV, led this coalition.

During the buildup to the 1998 election, new political parties emerged on the Right as well, including Proyecto Venezuela and Primero Justicia, but their core was made up of old members of AD and COPEI. The candidates who ran against Chávez generally all came out of the same tainted political background, and their attempts to build alliances against Chávez's coalition ended up embarrassing and discrediting both the parties and the candidates. Luis Alfaro Ucero represented AD; Irene Sáez represented her own party, but with initial support from COPEI; and Enrique Salas Romer represented Proyecto Venezuela, but at the last minute AD and COPEI switched their backing in the hopes of unifying the anti-Chávez vote behind Romer.

The traditional political parties maintained a strong national infrastructure that allowed them to win a respectable number of seats in the National Assembly and in the gubernatorial and mayoral elections under the new constitution in 2000. But the 2004 elections, the next national election of mayors and state governors, brought a serious defeat for the opposition political parties, indicative of a severe loss of popular support.

(7) What are the most significant structural changes that have occurred since Chávez was first elected?

Between 1999 and 2001, the most significant changes were political—the 1999 Bolivarian Constitution created a new political system designed to be broadly inclusive. The goal was to promote popular participation as a way of deepening and extending democracy beyond elections into all political issues. This political change (both the constitution and the new model of democracy have entire chapters dedicated to them below) also has implications for Venezuelan society, for the popular outlook, for political accountability, and for the extent to which people feel they, too, are stakeholders in the political system. Thus, in theory: popular participation leads to a change in the form of governing and holding public office because of a newfound accountability to the electorate through participatory mechanisms and the possibility of recall referenda.

In 2000, all branches of government underwent a relegitimization process in accordance with the new constitution, in which the people could either reelect or replace public officials. In this way the president, governors, mayors, members of the National Assembly, and even local representatives had to be reelected in order to govern under the new legal code. That same year, and in accordance with the new constitution, the bicameral legislature was replaced with a unicameral National Assembly—allowing for a streamlined legislative process that facilitates equal representation and participation, but that is also potentially easier for the executive branch to control.

Also in 2000, the government began a series of massive social plans to address the most urgent needs of Venezuela's poor. For example, Plan Bolívar 2000 drew on the strength and resources of the military to engage in natural disaster relief, urban renewal, the building of homes, and assistance with rural transportation.

In 2001, President Chávez issued forty-nine decrees under the temporary enabling Laws, which empowered him to legislate without going through the National Assembly (see question 28). These laws were intended to fulfill the requirements of the new constitution in a wide range of areas—including microfinance, hydrocarbons, land, sea, agrarian reform, government functioning, and industry—but became the rallying cry of the opposition in its efforts to overthrow the government. These laws directly challenged the interests of Venezuela's ruling class.

The Bolivarian government was actively consolidating its control over the state. As Chávez put it in an interview in 2002: "Up until now we have changed the macro political-legal structure, but because of the nature of our peaceful and profoundly democratic process, this structure is still marked by its old vices, infiltrated by adversaries; and sometimes our own ranks are infiltrated or weakened by loss of revolutionary consciousness."

In 2002, in the face of fierce resistance in the form of the short-lived coup d'état (discussed in chapter VI) and the national oil strike (see question 73), the government solidified its control over the state-run oil company, PDVSA. The company came under control of its parent Ministry of Energy and Mines, and President Chávez replaced the top executives with people loyal to his government. Thus, in 2003, relying on oil revenues, the government began to implement the massive social programs known as the missions. These programs (discussed in chapter V) continue today and have dramatically strengthened the government's popular base of support through initiatives that have nearly eradicated illiteracy and are providing free primary health care to all Venezuelans.

(8) **What problems has the revolution failed to resolve?**

Venezuela continues to be a poor, underdeveloped country. Meeting its citizens' basic needs is a central challenge for the Venezuelan government. Chávez himself has highlighted several areas in which his government has thus far failed to meet its goals.

President Chávez has made a point of being self-critical and has continually called on the people, and on elected officials throughout the country, to investigate and denounce any corruption or abuse of power. Chávez has said that between a million friends and a principle he will stick with his principle every time, citing the example of one of his oldest friends, Urdaneta Hernández, who was director of Venezuela's investigative police force (DISIP) when the force was implicated in a series of corruption scandals and abuses of power; Hernández lost his job and Chávez lost his friend.

President Chávez's promise to fight corruption notwithstanding, corruption in Venezuela continues and still plagues state institutions. According to Moisés Naím, editor in chief for *Foreign Policy* magazine, "Even though Chávez owes much of his political good fortune to his fiery anticorruption rhetoric and he enjoys almost completely unchecked leeway over almost all the levers of power, during his time in government corruption is still blatant and pervasive, and it still dominates everyone's minds." Former Prosecutor General Eduardo Roche Lander reported corruption in relation to the administration of Plan Bolívar 2000 funds.

This peaceful revolution has also failed to fix the inefficiency of the government bureaucracy. People throughout the country see President Chávez, rather than their local government officials, as the one person who is willing and able to solve their problems. This is, in part, because of his powerful, personal connection with the people, but also because of the real obstacle that bureaucracy continues to represent at almost every level of Venezuelan government. Despite the fact that the government has distributed free copies of essays like Che Guevara's *Against Bureaucracy*, the nature of government administration has changed all too little since the democratic revolution got under way six years ago.

One of President Chávez's commitments was to provide for all street children. Street children are not only one of the country's most vulnerable, excluded populations, but are also a symbol of the poverty that is still widespread in Venezuela. At a press conference on May 13, 2005, the Venezuelan government announced that it had begun providing three meals a day to all street children in the Bolivarian Schools, and in late July 2005, President Chávez announced the founding of a new mission to address the needs of street children. Nevertheless, street children are still a daily reality in Venezuelan cities, and the government has yet to develop a specific, concrete policy to end their desperate plight.

There are many other problems that the revolution has yet to resolve in terms of eradicating hunger and unemployment and providing quality housing, health care, and education. To its credit, the government is in the midst of what must inevitably be a long process, and it continues to develop new mechanisms to meet the most urgent needs of its citizens, such as the missions discussed in chapter V. In terms of these and other unresolved problems, Venezuelans have been patient as the Chávez government moves into its seventh year in office.

(9) Is this just another military government?

Some on the Left in Venezuela and beyond have rejected the Bolivarian Revolution because it is headed by a military man and because the military has played a prominent role in numerous state institutions and government plans. However, unlike in other countries in the region, or at other moments in Venezuelan history, during the more than six years in which the military has played a central role in the Venezuelan political scene, they have defended democratic processes and supported the people. This military orientation, unique in Latin America, can be explained by a series of factors that were formative for this generation of the Venezuelan military.

Beginning with Hugo Chávez's generation, most of the military's officers were not trained, as had been traditional, in the former School of the Americas in Fort Benning, Georgia—famous for the human rights abuses its graduates go on to commit. Rather, they were mostly trained in the Venezuelan Military Academy. In 1971, the Venezuelan Military Academy's curriculum was made consistent with nonmilitary university standards, and army cadres like Chávez began to study political science and to read about democracy and about Venezuelan history. Graduates often went to nonmilitary universities to specialize and build military-civilian networks. Moreover, this generation of military officers was trained after most of the country's guerrilla insurgency had dissolved or surrendered; thus, unlike so many other Latin American armed forces, they never fought an internal counterinsurgency. When Chávez and his generation of soldiers patrolled peasant zones in the interior, they came face-to-face with poverty, not a guerrilla force. Most senior officers and low-ranking troops alike are from poor urban and peasant families; they identify with the poor.

Another formative event for this generation of the military was the *Caracazo*—the social upheaval beginning on February 27, 1989. In response to the package of neoliberal economic measures imposed by the Carlos Andrés Pérez government, people from the poorest neighborhoods took to the streets and began setting buses on fire, looting trade centers, and destroying stores and supermarkets. The military came out to restore "order" and ended up massacring the protesters. Junior officers were furious that they had been ordered to turn their guns against their own people; this event shaped a new political awareness for many junior officers and led to the two failed coup attempts in 1992.

When Chávez was elected president in 1998, he concentrated on building strong relations between the people and the military, on converting the military from a domestic occupying army into a defense force with a social service focus. For the first time in Venezuelan history, the military has placed its energy, technical skills, and organizational knowledge at the service of the poorest sectors of society. The earliest example of this was Plan Bolívar 2000, which included cleaning up streets and schools, improving the environment, and renewing the social infrastructure in both urban and rural areas. The goal of the plan was to find solutions to social problems while generating employment in the neediest sectors and incorporating community organizations into these efforts. The plan had its share of problems and it was criticized for corruption and inefficiencies, but it represents the first major national social effort undertaken by the military.

Since then, the military joined forces with the masses to defend Venezuela's democracy during the April 2002 coup (discussed in chapter VI) and during the December 2002 oil strike (see question 73).

(10) **Are the changes in Venezuela truly revolutionary?**

In general, a revolution is a time of rapid, profound change. However, the word is inherently problematic because of its historical-political uses in a wide range of circumstances, for diverse sets of interests. Whether a process of change can actually be called a revolution depends to a large extent on what preexists that change. In a hunter-gatherer society, the introduction of simple planting techniques resulted in an "agricultural revolution." When agricultural societies developed basic mechanized systems of production, an industrial revolution was under way. When slaves in French Haiti rose up to seize their liberty and independence, forming their own government, they became political revolutionaries.

Prior to President Chávez's first election in 1998, Venezuela's government had been ruled by a two-party representative democratic regime for forty years. During that time the government administrated the country's resources in the interests of a small local elite, largely ignoring the needs of the vast majority of Venezuelans, so that by 1997 the wealthiest 5 percent of the population had incomes that were 53.1 times greater than the poorest 5 percent.[6] The election of President Chávez marked not only the end of a corrupt and predictable two-party system, but also the beginning of a rapid, profound, systematic process of change, which Chávez calls the Bolivarian Revolution. This peaceful, constitutional revolution is not only democratic in that it has been approved by popular votes at every step of the way, but it is also a revolution in democracy because it is in the process of creating the only participatory democracy in the hemisphere. Almost nowhere in the world are people at every level of society more engaged in the political process than they are in the streets, fields, and offices of Venezuela.

The Bolivarian Revolution began by overhauling the political-juridical structures that served to maintain the previous system of government and the rampant social inequalities that it produced. The revolution is now focusing on economic and social change in the interests of the majority of Venezuelans living in poverty and traditionally ignored by the government. These changes do not yet fundamentally impact capitalist development, the rule of law, or private property. Still, in the context of this country's recent history, most Venezuelans, whether they support them or oppose them, recognize that the profound changes that are currently in progress are indeed revolutionary.

International Relations

(11) What is the Venezuela-U.S. "battle of microphones"?

Since President Chávez's first election in 1998, and particularly since President Bush's first election in 2000, the bilateral rhetoric has become less and less diplomatic, and more and more hostile. The tit for tat of government spokespeople and officials has come to be known in Venezuela as the "battle of microphones." There are so many attacks and counterattacks, threats and recriminations that it would take a separate book to catalogue the "battle." Here is a selection of quotes from each side:

From the United States:

- Robert Zoellick, deputy secretary of state, in his confirmation hearing before the Senate Foreign Relations Committee, March 15, 2005:

  "Now, bringing this to Chávez: I think what you're seeing happening throughout the region is there's a new Pied Piper of Populism that's going on. So I don't look at it, Senator, as left or right. Because the first person who did this was Fujimori. So I don't know, is he right or left? And the same with Chávez."

- Porter Goss, director of the CIA, in testimony before the Senate Intelligence Committee, February 16, 2005:

    "In Venezuela, Chávez is consolidating his power by using technically legal tactics to target his opponents and meddling in the region supported by Castro."

- Marc Grossman, under secretary of state for political affairs, *El Tiempo*, Bogotá, February 15, 2005:

    "We believe that Venezuela is playing a negative role in the region and we will be watching very carefully what that country does. We prefer that they spend their money on development programs or on the war on terrorism."

- Secretary of State Condoleezza Rice (then head of the National Security Council), October 23, 2004, in the *Pittsburgh Tribune-Review*:

    "I think President Hugo Chávez is a real problem. I think he will continue to find ways to subvert democracy in his own country. He will continue to find ways to make his neighbors miserable."

- Roger Noriega, assistant secretary for the Bureau of Western Hemisphere Affairs, *La Voz de América*, April 6, 2004:

    "We are not intervening in internal affairs. We are cooperating with democratic elements in Venezuela in their constitutional activities to overcome the dangerous polarization that exists in Venezuela."

- Otto Reich, White House special envoy on Latin America, *El Tiempo*, Bogotá, March 6, 2004:

    "The person hurting the Venezuelan people [. . .] is the current president of Venezuela, who unfortunately is, apparently, trying to undermine the freedom of the Venezuelan people."

From Venezuela:

- President Hugo Chávez, May 22, 2005:

    "If they don't extradite [Luis Posada Carriles] in the time allowed in our [extradition] agreement, we will review our relations with the United States. . . . We would have to evaluate whether it is worth keeping an embassy in the United States and whether it is worth the United States having an embassy in Venezuela."

- President Hugo Chávez, February 20, 2005:

    "If they assassinate me, there will be one person to blame on this planet, and that person is the president of the United States, George W. Bush."

- President Hugo Chávez, February 17, 2005:

    "George W. Bush should be held responsible before the world for the deaths and blood that ran in Venezuela during the 2002 coup. U.S. military officials met with the coup plotters. The U.S. embassy congratulated them. His spokesman in Washington said that Chávez was a tyrant and it was necessary to support the new government."

- President Hugo Chávez, January 13, 2004:

    "Now [the United States] wants to impose the FTAA on us, without understanding that if they do, the governments won't be falling every year, but rather every day. The government in Washington should recognize that it is their neoliberal policies that destabilize, not Fidel or Chávez."

- President Hugo Chávez, June 10, 2003:

    "Mr. Bush: worry about the problems of the United States. Venezuela's problems are Venezuela's."

- Andrés Izarra, minister of communication and information, February 21, 2005:

    "We are sure that this kind of propaganda disguised as information, the kind that has recently formed a wave of aggression of more than forty-five articles, is part of a propaganda policy of the Bush administration."

(12) **What are Venezuela's new strategic alliances?**

Historically, Venezuelan governments have put a lot of energy into maintaining a strong relationship with the United States, without paying much attention to other bilateral relations or international alliances. This approach to foreign policy, not uncommon in Latin America and dating back to before the Monroe Doctrine, created a form of isolation and dependency. The Chávez government actively seeks ways to break that historic dependency. Since 1999, Venezuela has worked to deepen alliances in the region and pursued new relationships with countries all over the world. According to the Venezuelan government, many of these new alliances run much deeper than the simple signing of trade pacts and actually represent steps toward regional and international solidarity.

Chávez works to realize Simón Bolívar's dream of Latin American integration in the interests of defending the welfare and sovereignty of the region. To that end, Chávez meets with the presidents of Brazil, Argentina, and Cuba several times a year. Venezuela and Brazil—the economic heavyweight with a massive industrial base—have signed a series of economic, energy, telecommunications, and military treaties. Venezuela and Argentina have signed mutual-support treaties, including one in which Venezuela agreed to buy nearly $1 billion in bonds to help Argentina recover from its financial crisis of 2001. In defiance of the U.S.-led blockade, Venezuela has negotiated preferential prices for Cuba's oil imports in exchange for services, technology, and the use of thousands of doctors and medicine to Venezuela's poor through Mission Barrio Adentro (see question 42). Venezuela has also signed a series of treaties that provide preferential buying conditions for many of its neighbors, thus dramatically increasing its oil exports in the region (see question 75). In February 2005, Venezuela cancelled the small Caribbean island of Dominica's debt and donated more than $10 million in development aid. Venezuela has also led in the integration of the two most important South American economic blocks—the Andean Community of Nations (CAN) and the Southern Common Market (Mercosur) to form the South American Community of Nations.

Venezuela's foreign policy goes beyond its regional alliances. Before President Chávez was elected, Venezuela had stopped any meaningful participation in OPEC, preferring lower prices for oil and higher export volume. In 1999 President Chávez set off on a historic tour of ten of the leading members of OPEC, including controversial visits to Saddam Hussein in Iraq and to Mu'ammar Gadhafi in Libya. Then, in 2000, Venezuela hosted an OPEC summit in which it successfully strengthened the entire oil cartel; the country was selected president of the organization and began to drive world market prices up. Since then, Venezuela has continued to dedicate time and energy to maintaining its relationship with OPEC member states, and President Chávez has returned to visit his allies in the Middle East on several occasions. In early 2005, Venezuela hosted President Khatami of Iran, and gave tours of the missions and other social programs to a Saudi minister.

After putting its relationships with other oil-exporting countries in order and gaining meaningful control of the state oil company, PDVSA (discussed in chapter VIII), Venezuela began to develop its relationships with rising economic powers around the world. President Chávez has cultivated his relationship with China, visiting this economic mammoth on several separate trips and signing numerous economic agreements. For example, the Chinese and the Venezuelans have partnered in a joint venture to install a plant for the China Petroleum Co. in the Orinoco River basin to produce four million tons of superheavy crude oil by 2008, all for Chinese consumption. Venezuela has also begun buying uniforms for its army and other low-cost imports from China.

In March 2005, President Chávez visited India to sign cultural and economic agreements and to pave the way for oil exports to one of Asia's largest energy consumers.

Through this diverse, complex series of economic, social, and energy agreements, Venezuela has developed a strong, independent foreign policy, much to the chagrin of the U.S. government. Finally, Venezuela has used a series of strategic arms purchases to strengthen old alliances and build new ones.

(13) Is Venezuela starting a regional arms race?

After President Chávez visited Russia in late 2004, he announced that negotiations were under way to buy 100,000 rifles to replace the standard-issue rifles—decades-old Belgian FALs—of the armed forces. The deal also includes transport helicopters and the purchase of the technology to produce the rifles and munitions locally. Then, in February 2005, Venezuela announced plans to buy twenty-four Tucano patrol planes from Brazil. Spain also announced its intention to sell coastal patrol vessels and transport planes to Venezuela—none of them have offensive capacities.

The U.S. government has lambasted this arms buildup for having the potential to cause a regional arms race, for clandestinely serving to provide guerrilla groups in Colombia with small arms, or for being a means to export the Bolivarian Revolution to other countries in the region. President Bush, Secretary of Defense Donald Rumsfeld, and Secretary of State Condoleezza Rice have all personally expressed their opposition to these arms deals. As President Bush explained in a press conference on May 5, 2005, "We made our position very clear on the AK-47s to Venezuela, and that is, is that we're concerned that those weapons could end up in the hands of FARC, for example, a very destabilizing force in South America." Or, according to Secretary Rice, on April 20, 2005: "Well, I think that the question is not about Russian arms, it's about the Venezuelan regime and what we've always talked about is troublesome behavior. The Venezuelan regime, I guess, one would ask the question, you know, what's the purpose of this weapons purchase? But we understand that the Russians sell arms. We didn't accuse them of violating anything. In fact, that's not the point." The point seems to be that the U.S. government feels uncomfortable with Venezuela acquiring even light arms.

The arms purchases serve a range of purposes for the Venezuelan government. First, the armed forces equipment has not been updated for years, and certain basic materials, such as planes and rifles, are in decay. Venezuela's aging fleet of U.S.-made F-16s is in need of replacement parts; the U.S. government will not authorize their sale. Instead of continuing its total military dependence on the United States, Venezuela has begun to diversify its arms suppliers.

Both Colombia and the United States have criticized Venezuela for failing to secure its long border from the incursion of Colombian armed groups, drug-smuggling cartels, and human-trafficking networks. The Tucano propeller planes, the patrol boats, and the transport planes are intended for use patrolling its long border with Colombia. Although U.S. government spokespeople have expressed concern over the potential for these purchases to cause a regional arms race, it is hard to take these claims seriously in light of the several billions of dollars of military aid, including high-technology weapons with offensive capacities, that the U.S. government has given Colombia since 1999 under Plan Colombia. Likewise, U.S. concerns about the weapons falling into the hands of illegal armed groups are ironic: in May 2005, Colombian officials arrested several active-duty members of the U.S. military stationed in Colombia for trying to sell tens of thousands of rounds of ammunition to Colombian paramilitary groups. The

ammunition had been brought into Colombia as part of the U.S. military aid
to the government, and naturally President Chávez took the opportunity to
lambaste the United States for its hypocrisy.

(14) Why is Venezuela opposed to the Free Trade Area of the Americas (FTAA)?

The FTAA is a project conceived and backed by the United States to make all
of the Western Hemisphere (thirty-four countries), with the exception of
Cuba, a free-trade zone. After seeing the initial success of the North American Free Trade Association (NAFTA) for U.S. corporate interests, the
United States launched the idea for the FTAA with a meeting of representatives from all thirty-four countries in Miami in December 1994. The agreement that came out of that initial round of negotiations established January
2005 as the target date for implementing the FTAA. All of the countries,
including Venezuela, agreed to the initial timeline. The first meeting that
President Chávez attended on this topic was held in Quebec City, Canada, in
2001. At that meeting Venezuela was the only country that expressed reser-
vations about the viability of meeting the January 2005 implementation
target date.

The FTAA represents a top-down model of economic integration. More
than just a free-trade agreement, it would reduce the sovereignty of countries
by restraining their ability to act against multinational corporations. Given
the history of neoliberal policy in Venezuela, it is hard to imagine any
Venezuelan government supporting the FTAA. For Venezuela, the idea of
opening its markets to the United States is less attractive than it is to other
Latin American countries, because Venezuela's primary export, oil, would
not benefit significantly from the kind of trade liberalization the FTAA
promises. Venezuela's oil economy makes it a large importer and small
exporter of the nonpetroleum products that other Latin American countries
depend on as exports. Venezuela's earlier implementation of International
Monetary Fund (IMF) liberalization policies in the 1980s led to a dramatic
increase in poverty, a widening of the gap between the rich and the poor, the
de-industrialization of the country, and ultimately a national political crisis.

President Chávez has opposed the FTAA more strongly than any other
leader in the region. The FTAA is not the right choice for Latin America,

but is rather a representation of North America's strategic economic inter-ests in the region. NAFTA represents increased profits for international cor-porations and serious attacks against organized labor, artisans, and local producers; it has increased poverty and socioeconomic inequality. The con-cept of "free trade" between a global power like the United States and coun-tries as poor and isolated as most of those in the region is questionable.

In comparison with the United States, all Latin American countries, with the possible exception of Brazil, show up to the meetings in extremely weak negotiating positions. For this reason, various Latin American coun-tries have expressed interest in negotiating as blocks such as Mercosur. Chávez argues that before negotiating economic integration with the United States, multilateral Latin American economic integration should be further strengthened. Chávez and the Bolivarian Constitution demand that any major integration proposals be submitted to popular referenda before being implemented.

Other countries, such as Brazil, also opposed the FTAA because, in spite of its "free trade" rhetoric, the United States continues to provide some of the world's highest agricultural subsidies to its own farmers, thus under-mining one of the few sectors in which Latin American countries would oth-erwise have a competitive advantage. Brazil's and Venezuela's opposition made the realization of the FTAA in 2005 impossible. Nonetheless, Brazil, by far South America's largest economy, has expressed its interest in moving forward with negotiations if the United States is willing to cut back its domestic agricultural subsidies.

(15) Why has there been tension between Venezuela and Colombia?

Venezuela and Colombia share a long history and, along with Ecuador, they formed part of the Spanish colony that Simón Bolívar hoped to unite into "La Gran Colombia." Bolívar's dream did not work out; ever since 1830, when La Gran Colombia split into separate states, Colombia and Venezuela have followed two different trajectories.

Colombia has tended toward conservative governments and a radical, left-wing armed resistance. In Colombia both left- and right-wing armed groups have proliferated since the 1950s, leading to devastating ongoing low-intensity civil war. Venezuela, on the other hand, has tended toward liberal governments, and although it also went through a period of armed struggle between radical left-wing guerrillas and the government in the 1960s, since then it has not suffered a civil war.

The bilateral relationship between these neighbors has suffered because of Colombia's ongoing armed conflict, which has displaced millions of people over the years—hundreds of thousands of them seeking refuge in neighboring countries, including Venezuela. Colombia's multidimensional war includes extensive drug trafficking, terrorism, kidnapping, paramilitaries, guerrillas, and widespread human rights abuses. It is also a war in which the United States has increasingly played a role—primarily through billions of dollars of military aid to the Colombian government. In 2000 Colombia became the third-largest beneficiary of U.S. military aid in the world, after Israel and Egypt.

Although the war in Colombia has nothing to do with Venezuela, both Colombia and the United States have encouraged Venezuelan involvement in fighting the armed groups operating along their porous border. For example, in a press conference on October 5, 2004, in Bogotá, General James Hill, then in charge of the U.S. Southern Command, said that the Colombian war should include neighboring countries in the region, and that he hoped Venezuela would play its part. Venezuela has decided to remain uninvolved in Colombia's civil war and has, on several occasions, offered to serve as a mediator in possible peace negotiations. Meanwhile, Venezuela has stationed more than twenty thousand troops in border zones and, as discussed above, has begun to acquire light weaponry to better patrol its border.

Despite its declared neutrality, Venezuela has been accused of collaborating with the Colombian guerrillas. There is no evidence to support these claims. In December 2004, Rodrigo Granda, a high-ranking representative of the Fuerzas Armadas Revolucionarias de Colombia (FARC), Colombia's largest illegal armed group, was kidnapped in Caracas and handed over to Colombian officials. The kidnapping brought Colombia and Venezuela to the verge of war, and representatives of the U.S. State Department expressed their "100 percent support for Colombia." Colombia and the United States claimed that Venezuela was aiding and abetting a known terrorist; Venezuela claimed its sovereignty had been violated and that no official request for Granda's extradition arrived until after his kidnapping on Venezuelan soil. Although trade was temporarily cut off between Venezuela and Colombia,

Fidel Castro's diplomatic intervention led to an easing of tensions in February 2005.

Colombia's civil war leads to numerous other problems for Venezuela. Venezuela and Colombia share a 1,400-mile-long border, mainly consisting of Amazon jungle and other territory that is difficult to control. Venezuela is used as a transit country for drug and human trafficking, and U.S. State Department human rights reports have cited Venezuela for failures in these areas. These are international crimes that Venezuela has an obligation to combat, yet Venezuela is mainly used as a transit country for criminal groups operating out of Colombia.

Despite these difficulties, Colombia and Venezuela continue to be each other's second-largest trading partners (after the United States). Venezuelan-Colombian trade is expected to reach a record $5 billion in 2005, including the project under way to develop an oil pipeline that will carry Venezuelan oil to Pacific ports in Colombia. This significant economic relationship has created the impetus for rapid resolution of conflicts like the Granda affair.

(16) Does Chávez's government ally with "terrorist" governments?

The Venezuelan government has relationships with governments around the world, including some that the Bush administration has deemed to be part of the "axis of evil." Venezuela maintains a foreign policy independent of the U.S. State Department and refuses to allow Washington to determine which countries it will or will not work with. The U.S. government has criticized its bilateral relations with countries such as Cuba, Libya, and Iran.

President Chávez and Fidel Castro have become close friends, and their countries have strong relations in areas such as education, health, culture, and trade. Under President Chávez's leadership, these relations have dramatically expanded, in spite of the U.S. embargo against Cuba. Venezuela and Cuba have signed bilateral treaties on mutual assistance in areas such as sports training, medical services, and educational assistance, including some twenty thousand Cuban doctors working in Venezuela, and Venezuelan students studying in Cuba.

Oil has been key to the development of Venezuela's relationships with Libya, Iran, and Iraq. In light of the crucial role oil plays in Venezuela's economy, President Chávez has improved relations with members of OPEC through official state visits, invitations to Venezuela, and commercial treaties. On his OPEC tour in 2000, Chávez became the first elected head of state to visit Iraq since the 1991 Persian Gulf War. He had to enter over land from Iran because of the U.S./UK no-fly zone enforced over most of Iraqi territory. President Chávez made this trip despite the protests of the U.S. government. Richard Boucher, the spokesman for the U.S. State Department, called this visit "particularly irritating." Then, in 2002, Venezuela opposed the U.S. invasion of Iraq, and continues to criticize the United States for the death of over 100,000 civilians and for its false claims of weapons of mass destruction to justify the war.

When President Chávez visited Mu'ammar Gadhafi of Libya in November 2004, he was awarded the Mu'ammar Gadhafi Human Rights Prize. When, in March 2005, President Khatami of Iran visited Venezuela, Chávez called him a brother and expressed his support for Iran's right to develop nuclear technology. Chávez announced his interest in developing nuclear energy sources on May 22, 2005, and suggested that Iran might cooperate with Venezuela to that end. He stressed that he had no interest in nuclear weaponry, but analysts question the wisdom of a country with some of the world's largest energy reserves (including oil, natural gas, coal, and hydroelectric power) investing in nuclear energy.

Venezuela has a right to maintain diplomatic relations with any country it chooses, and the realpolitik norm in international relations is that countries choose their alliances primarily based on national interest rather than on any sort of enlightened system of values. Still, Venezuela has cultivated economic relationships with countries, particularly with other members of OPEC, that have dismal human rights records and political values that are far removed from the ideals established in the Bolivarian Constitution. Venezuela's decision to do business in particular cases seems inconsistent with its stated goal of solidarity with the downtrodden the world over.

(17) What do people mean when they talk about an oil foreign policy?

Petroleum products are the largest and most valuable of Venezuela's exports. Moreover, petroleum products have strategic significance in the global economy. This means that the state oil company, PDVSA, and the oil industry as a whole play a key role in Venezuela's foreign policy, just as they do domestically. The relationship between the state oil industry and foreign policy was made explicit in 2004, when Alí Rodríguez Araque was promoted from president of PDVSA to foreign minister.

Well before that political appointment, one could talk about an oil foreign policy because President Chávez made relations with other OPEC countries such a high priority. In the same way, the Caracas Energy Cooperation Accord's extension of preferential oil sales to Central American and Caribbean countries (see question 75), and the development of Petroamérica are examples of Venezuela's use of its oil to gain ground in other areas of foreign policy. Oil has also been central to Venezuela's improved relations with rising global economic powers like Russia, China, and India.

Venezuela's independent oil foreign policy combined with the fact that it continues to be one of the United States' largest suppliers of oil is, perhaps, responsible for a fair amount of the tension between these two countries. It is the risk of losing its virtual monopoly on such a reliable supply of an important natural resource that leads so many U.S. policy makers to worry about Venezuela's internal political developments. Oil has made it possible for Venezuela to survive in the midst of a world that is hostile to its political experiment. Oil is what forces the United States to take this Latin American country as seriously as it does Kuwait, Saudi Arabia, and Iraq. And it is oil, together with a strong foreign policy and a series of innovative social programs and endogenous development, that is providing a higher quality of life for the vast majority of Venezuelans.

(18) How does Venezuela prioritize relations with Latin American countries?

President Chávez's prioritization of relations with his Latin American and Caribbean neighbors is clear in his Bolivarian rhetoric as well as in his actions. Broadly speaking, Chávez is trying to use Latin American integration to shift the regional balance of power. This was Simón Bolívar's dream, too, as President Chávez is quick to remind his listeners.

For Chávez, Latin American integration is a broad, multifaceted project. It is economic because it seeks ways to combine markets, share experience and technology, and work on joint ventures. It is political because it establishes the mechanisms and the trust to confront regional challenges as a group rather than as small, weak, isolated countries. It is cultural because of the shared history of the region and because, despite the real differences, Latin America has one common identity when considered globally. It is militaristic because it implies the capacity to coordinate the region's numerous armed forces to protect and defend their collective interests rather than depending on and being vulnerable to foreign armies.

With these goals and the general improvement of regional relations in mind, President Chávez has met with the presidents of Brazil, Argentina, and Cuba several times a year. Through these meetings, and others in the region, Venezuela has launched a series of specific regional-integration projects.

Since Venezuela is an oil-exporting country, it is pursuing the idea of forming a regional oil company that would be called "Petroamérica" and that would bring together the state oil companies from Argentina, Brazil, and Venezuela (see question 74). Another one of President Chávez's regional integration projects is the new continental news network called Telesur (see question 65). President Chávez sees these programs in energy, communications, and trade as imperative for an independent and strong Latin America.

(19) Why has Venezuela positioned itself as a leader among developing countries?

Venezuela's domestic policies depend on a strong, independent foreign policy that leads toward a multipolar world. Venezuela is initiating a set of diverse, extraordinary alliances in order to break its historic dependence on the United States, thus proving it is possible to maintain an independent foreign and domestic model. On various international issues impacting poor countries, Venezuela has taken a leadership role, and Chávez is now seen as one of the few political leaders in the world who has fought for independent government policies in the face of tremendous U.S. pressure. Moreover, he has confronted the United States at almost every opportunity through a policy that—for those who support him—represents speaking truth to power, and—for those who oppose him—represents populist anti-Americanism. Many of the poor people in the world, certainly in Latin America, are tired of having their governments promise one thing and deliver another, always representing the interests of the local elite. For these people, the concrete achievements of the Venezuelan government, including the political will to fight poverty, have made Chávez a regional and even a global leader.

During 2005 Venezuela took steps to open permanent diplomatic channels with a series of African countries, and Chávez is planning an African diplomatic tour. This represents the first-ever Venezuelan diplomatic effort in Africa.

Chávez has not only improved relations with other poor countries, but also with people and movements the world over. He has used his speeches criticizing the neoliberal economic model and calling for an international humanitarian fund at several key international summits, such as the FTAA in Quebec in 2001, Sustainable Development in Johannesburg in 2002, the Americas in Monterrey in 2004, and the World Social Forum in Porto Alegre in 2005. During his world tours, Chávez makes time for meetings with intellectuals, such as the group of professors at Jawaharlal Nehru University in India, with labor movements, such as the Madrid Labor Union in Spain, and with social movements such as the Landless Workers' Movement in Brazil.

(20) What are the primary weaknesses and strengths of Venezuela's foreign policy?

Venezuela has serious weaknesses in its foreign policy. Particularly under President Chávez's leadership, bilateral relations with its two most important neighbors—Colombia and the United States—have deteriorated drastically. Since Venezuela continues to depend on its relations with these two countries, the fact that bilateral tensions have increased is a significant failure in Venezuelan foreign policy. This situation is not the sole responsibility of the Venezuelan government, as its decisions have been made in the context of hostility from these countries and their allies in Venezuela.

The Ministry of the Exterior has yet to come fully under the control of the government, and many of the bureaucrats and low-level diplomats in this ministry are opposed to the government's Bolivarian project. To combat this weakness, the government has taken a series of measures, including appointing a new minister and vice ministers, and establishing a Presidential Office for International Relations, but these actions have yet to impact all levels of the ministry or to make it unnecessary. In an area as crucial as its foreign policy, Venezuela does not count on a loyal, determined core of people who will effectively represent government policies to the rest of the world.

Venezuela has demonstrated success in stopping, at least temporarily, the implementation of the FTAA despite U.S. pressure and efforts to implement it by January 2005. The delay of the FTAA is related to a number of factors, but certainly President Chávez's efforts, including his promotion of the Bolivarian Alternative for the Americas (ALBA), played a role.

Since President Chávez was first elected, the world has witnessed the rapid rise of the Left throughout Latin America. Brazil, Uruguay, and Argentina now all have left-of-center governments with popular bases of support. These other governments have all, thus far, chosen a more moderate path than Venezuela's, and their rise to power is due, primarily, to internal circumstances in the context of continental and global forces. Nonetheless, the Venezuelan model and the hope that it gives to poor and marginalized people has strengthened leftist parties and movements throughout the region. In turn, the rise of the Left in Latin America has allowed Venezuela's regional integration policies to make significant advances, including the developments toward Petroamérica and Telesur.

Most recently, Venezuela has won a series of small but significant diplomatic victories in the Organization of American States (OAS). In the spring of 2005, prior to the elections for secretary general of this regional organization, Venezuela backed the Chilean, José Miguel Insulza, while the United States backed the former Salvadoran president Francisco Flores. Before the election, Flores withdrew from the race and the United States switched its support to the third candidate, Luis Ernesto Derbez of Mexico. After much political maneuvering, the United States was forced to support Insulza to avoid outright embarrassment. It was the first time the United States' firstchoice candidate has not won since the organization was founded in 1948.

In June 2005 at the general assembly meeting of the OAS held in Florida, the United States pushed for a resolution that would allow the organization to "monitor democracies throughout the region." It was seen as an attempt to criticize the Venezuelan government and, in a clear defeat for the Bush administration, the OAS agreed on a watered-down version of a U.S.-backed proposal. Diplomats reached a compromise between U.S. demands for greater accountability and Latin America's belief in the "principle of nonintervention" upon which the organization was established. Latin American nations managed to get the final OAS declaration to reflect their concerns that continuing poverty, even after a decade of economic reforms, represented one of the greatest threats to democracy. Likewise, a statement was added affirming that "all countries have the right to decide their own 'political status' and economic, social and cultural development."

The strengths of Venezuela's foreign policy are not limited to Latin America. One of President Chávez's first successes in foreign relations was the relaunching of OPEC (see question 78), a success that has made the rest of Venezuela's domestic and foreign policies possible.

The New Constitution

(21) **What was the significance of the change from the Fourth to the Fifth Republic?**

Venezuela's First Republic was founded with the declaration of independence from Spain on April 19, 1811, and the implementation of Venezuela's first constitution that same year. This republic lasted just one year, until General Francisco de Miranda surrendered to the Spanish imperial army in July 1812. The Second Republic began with the triumph of Simón Bolívar over Spanish forces on August 6, 1813, and ended in December 1814, when imperial forces defeated the patriots at the battles of Urica and Maturin. The Third Republic began in 1817 with the restoration of the state institutions in Guyana and ended with the Congress of Angostura in 1819, where the union of Bolívar's La Gran Colombia was formalized and Venezuela briefly became a part of this larger republic. The Fourth Republic began in 1830, when La Gran Colombia separated into the independent republics of Ecuador, Colombia, and Venezuela.

The change from the Fourth to the Fifth Republic refers specifically to the change in the form of government that occurred with the promulgation of the 1999 Constitution of the Bolivarian Republic of Venezuela. Naming the government the Fifth Republic serves an explicitly political purpose in that it draws on the symbolism of the independence movement that led to the founding of the country's first republics.

President Chávez argues that in order to construct a state with the capacity to provide Venezuelans with the greatest possible access to happiness, justice, and social equality, it was necessary to develop a new legal code. Upon taking office, he called for a national referendum to determine whether or not to hold a constitutional assembly in which the people could express their sovereign right to change the nation's political system from below by rewriting the constitution.

The opposition to Chávez and his political process based on the new constitution has disputed his presentation of the history and politics every step of the way. Opposition intellectuals view his Fifth Republic rhetoric as nothing more than political hyperbole, though the idea has taken hold in most public discourse.

(22) Why did Venezuela write a new constitution?

Since the 1990s, President Chávez had argued for the need for a constitutional assembly. During his first presidential campaign he promised that, if elected, he would call for a constitutional assembly to rewrite the republic's constitution. Thus, millions of Venezuelans came to expect a constitutional assembly, and when President Chávez initiated it, he fulfilled his first major promise to the electorate. As he puts it, Venezuela rewrote its constitution "in order to refound the republic, to relegitimize public power and to create a new democracy."[7]

The previous Magna Carta represented the interests of the old political ruling class, their elitism, their corruption, and their exclusionary practices, and it had become an obstacle to the development of a new, participatory model of democracy. In the statement of legislative intent for the new constitution, its drafters wrote: "It is no longer just the state's responsibility to be democratic, but also society's responsibility. All of the elements that make up a democratic society should also be based on democratic principles."

President Chávez's strategy was to break with the country's political traditions, which had become defined by the failures and vices of the previous forty years of power-sharing between the two dominant parties. The 1999

Bolivarian Constitution was a way of starting over. Chávez's political goals would not have been possible without totally overhauling the state structure and legal code: by legally and democratically rewriting the constitution, he opened the way for the major social and economic changes that are at the heart of his political agenda.

(23) What was the legal process for writing and passing the new constitution?

The constitutional assembly, convened through a national referendum, was charged with writing the new constitution. The assembly was composed of 131 members chosen by the people in national elections. The alliance supporting Chávez won 125 seats in the election and the national constitutional assembly was formally opened on August 3, 1999. On August 5, President Chávez presented a draft for a new constitution. He recommended that the members create a strong state, capable of governing and meeting the ample needs of its people. He spoke against the neoliberal theory dominant in the rest of Latin America and in favor of his vision of equality, justice, and social development.

The process of writing the text of the new constitution, based on the template that President Chávez presented to the assembly, was not limited to the members elected to the assembly, but rather was open to public participation through individual committees that made up the assembly and that were charged with incorporating the ideas generated by the public into particular thematic-based sections of the new constitution. The full assembly came together to incorporate the recommendations and drafts of each committee into the final document.

Public participation took many forms, including forums, Internet pages, popular assemblies, study groups, and public debates. The privately owned media, universities, political parties, and NGOs all brought their suggestions to the attention of the members of the assembly elected from their region, who were then charged with delivering the ideas to the relevant subcommittee.

The drafting of the constitution lasted roughly three months. According to President Chávez, it was necessary to write the constitution quickly since "a long debate would have impeded the ongoing political process" and the government's ability to fulfill its campaign promises. However, expediting the process of writing and approving the constitution limited the amount of public debate and participation.

Despite this flaw, the process was relatively transparent, and no one committee had free rein to write independently of the public or of the other committees. For example, the health committee had the right to read and comment on the work in progress of any of the other committees, and vice versa. This made it possible for each committee to draw on, participate in, and learn from the process under way in each of the other committees.

Once the draft was completed, the final document had to be approved by referendum before it replaced the old constitution. Thus, the assembly had millions of copies printed and distributed for public debate. Finally, in December 1999, a national referendum was held to approve or reject the newly drafted Bolivarian Constitution. It was approved with approximately 88 percent of the vote, though less than 38 percent of eligible voters turned out.

(24) Does the new constitution guarantee human rights and civil rights?

Article 19 of the constitution says: "The State shall guarantee to every individual, in accordance with progressive principles and without discrimination of any kind, nonwaivable, indivisible and interdependent enjoyment and exercise of human rights. Respect for and the guaranteeing of these rights is obligatory for the organs of Public Power, in accordance with the Constitution, the human rights treaties signed and ratified by the Republic, and any laws developing the same."

Title III of the constitution (on duties, human rights, and guarantees) includes more than 100 articles directly addressing a wide range of human and civil rights. These rights are organized by category, including: nationality and citizenship, political rights and public referenda, social and family rights, cultural and educational rights, economic rights, rights of native peoples, and environmental rights. Since the constitution was written recently, its authors attempted to integrate the latest in international standards for human rights, including not only basic human rights such as those pertaining to civil freedoms (freedom of speech, freedom of religion, freedom of political association), which are basically political and civil rights, but also economic, social, and cultural rights more related to equality. The constitution guarantees all citizens access to education, to health care, and to dignified housing. In other words, the rights established in the International Covenant on Economic, Social, and Cultural Rights (ICESC) are entrenched in the Bolivarian Constitution. The constitution also recognizes and protects group rights and collective rights, such as those of indigenous peoples, whose rights are delineated in chapter VIII of the new constitution.

Still, the constitution has been criticized for guaranteeing more than the state can—or should—provide its citizens. Thus, the issue of how to develop laws that enforce these rights has become more and more problematic.

The opposition has criticized the constitution for, among other things, concentrating too much power in the executive branch and for limiting freedom of speech in article 57, which reads as follows: "Everyone has the right to express freely his or her thoughts, ideas, or opinions orally, in writing or by any other form of expression, and to use for such purpose any means of communication and diffusion, and no censorship shall be established. Anyone making use of this right assumes full responsibility for everything expressed. Anonymity, war propaganda, discriminatory messages, or those promoting religious intolerance are not permitted." For many critics, the last two sentences of the article represent an unacceptable limit on the freedom of speech.

Human rights groups and the private media in Venezuela have also expressed their concerns over article 58: "Everyone has the right to timely, truthful, and impartial information, without censorship. . . ." Critics have objected to the positive obligation this line imposes on the media, and fear that it may be used to justify excessive state limitations on the media.

In addition to the criticisms mentioned above, article 67, which eliminates public financing for political parties (as part of the trend toward a non-party-based democracy), has drawn criticisms. According to some, such as Margarita López Maya, a Venezuelan writer and social scientist, this article weakens the ability of political organizations representative of sectors without resources to compete with more powerful interest groups. While this is a legitimate concern, given the shift away from party politics since the promulgation of the new constitution, it has yet to present itself as a major issue.

(25) **Is this constitution really innovative?**

The participatory process through which the constitution was established is innovative. For one of the few times in modern history, a constitution was developed with massive popular participation and approved by popular vote, resulting in a document that was broad enough to include the rights, needs, and ideals of almost every social group within Venezuelan society. In the 1991 constitutional assembly in Colombia, a minority of political interests were able to control the process. In Venezuela, the people not only participated in the drafting process but also had the opportunity to cast their ballots to approve or reject the final document.

But beyond the methodology through which it was written and approved, the constitution is innovative because its contents reflect the social inclusion and political will to move the country toward a model of sustainable development based on local resources and needs. Rather than simply establishing the framework for a system of government, this constitution goes into great detail about the kind of economy, social system, and cultural values that the state should promote. With regard to the political system, the constitution de-emphasizes the role of political parties, focusing on the role of the people and civil society groups. Of course, this level of specificity makes the constitution not only innovative, but also controversial.

When people talk about the inclusive nature of the constitution, they are referring specifically to efforts to include groups largely cut out of the previous system of government—women, children, indigenous peoples, the unemployed, and the elderly. Inclusion of these groups was reflected not only in the content of the articles, but also in the language used throughout. For example, in Spanish, words that refer to both men and women are given the masculine ending. In the Bolivarian Constitution, however, both the feminine and masculine words are used throughout as a way to break through the sexism and machismo built into the language. International women's rights groups have praised the constitution because of article 88: "The State guarantees the equality and equitable treatment of men and women in the exercise of the right to work. The State recognizes work at home as an economic activity that creates added value and produces social welfare and wealth. Housewives are entitled to Social Security in accordance with the law." With this article, the Bolivarian Constitution goes further than any other constitution in the world to recognize and defend women's rights.

Finally, the constitution goes so far as to change the name of the country from the Republic of Venezuela to include *El Libertador*'s last name: The Bolivarian Republic of Venezuela. Although this is largely rhetorical, for

80% of minimum wage
for women. subsistence wage

most Venezuelans it is only fitting that the name of *El Libertador*, which graces the currency and the main avenue and plaza in every town, also be included in the name of the country.

(26) How was the new constitution received outside of Venezuela?

The authors of the Bolivarian Constitution made it consistent with international law, including the International Covenant on Civil and Political Rights, the International Covenant on Economic, Social, and Cultural Rights, and the Convention on the Rights of the Child, which resulted in a document that has been widely recognized for its conformance with international human rights law. Despite this effort to integrate international human rights covenants, outside observers have raised several criticisms of the new constitution.

Commentators have expressed concern about the amount of power given to the executive branch, and about the fact that its limitations on the state's ability to privatize national industries will result in a loss of international investment. Others express their concern that the social guarantees it provides are not realistic.

People supporting the constitution also tend to focus on the section guaranteeing human rights and civil rights. Organizations such as the Caribbean Amerindian Centrelink have praised the constitution for the advances it makes in terms of indigenous rights, suggesting that it is unparalleled in this area. At the Indigenous Summit at the Americas Social Forum, indigenous groups from all over the hemisphere passed a resolution supporting the constitution for its passages prioritizing indigenous rights.

International jurists have recognized the Bolivarian Constitution for its extraordinary protections. Much of the criticism the constitution has received reflects the concerns of the Venezuelan opposition with regard to the true intentions of the document and the Chávez government in general. Many initial concerns have already been proven false, such as the claim that the recall referendum would never be used against President Chávez himself. Nonetheless, like any juridical document, it is not just the content that matters, but also how the government implements it. This has been and will continue to be the most important test for the Bolivarian Constitution.

(27) **Have the Venezuelan people accepted the new constitution as their own?**

Jesus Gilberto Rojas, a sociologist working for the municipal government in Sucre, Venezuela, describes a trip he took with two German visitors to a small coastal community. One of the Germans asked the people they met if they felt alienated by the national government. A member of the community responded by pulling out a pocket-sized copy of the Bolivarian Constitution and pointing out that it detailed their rights in housing, labor, political participation, and more. This response can only be seen as normal in a country where citizens understand that their constitution is a tool that should be used to defend their rights. As this anecdote illustrates, in Venezuela, the Bolivarian Constitution has indeed become a part of daily life.

In *The Revolution Will Not Be Televised*, one of the many video documentaries recorded during the April 2002 coup, a homemaker, constitution in hand, expresses her outrage at the detention of President Chávez: "And what are they going to do with my vote? I voted for Chávez and I want him to finish his term."

More generally, all Venezuelan schools include the constitution in their curriculum. Students are regularly assigned research projects involving the application of the rights guaranteed in the constitution. Community and state TV, such as Catia TV or Vive, air successful programs in which citizens are presented with a legal problem and are asked to use the constitution to try to resolve it.

The government has campaigned to make the constitution a part of daily life and encouraged people to feel ownership over it. Even members of the opposition, who originally refused to even accept the idea of a new constitution, have come to cite it in their efforts to agitate for change. Julio Borges, for example, a leading member of the Primero Justicia Party, and as this book went to print the only declared opposition candidate for the 2006 presidential elections, dedicates his weekly column in the largest circulating daily, *Últimas Noticias*, to informing his readers about their constitutional rights and about legal instruments useful to average citizens that are built into the Bolivarian Constitution. Other members of the opposition can regularly be seen on TV, or are quoted in the news, declaring their opinion on controversial articles or clauses.

Chávez himself always carries a copy of this little blue book, small enough to fit into his shirt pocket. In his appearances on TV, he is regularly seen pulling out his constitution and quoting from it, both as an example to the people of how to draw on the constitution and as a way of educating them about specific rights and responsibilities.

Since the final version was distributed and implemented, it has gone on to become one of the most widely read books in Venezuelan history—according to some estimates on par with the Bible. Because most of the versions sold are printed and distributed by street vendors in the informal sector of the economy, it is hard to get accurate estimates of the total number sold, but many put the number of Bolivarian Constitutions printed since its 1999 approval at around eight million copies. Considering that Venezuela has a population of twenty-five million people, this means that more than one constitution has been sold for each family in the country. The constitution has been widely translated, not only into English, French, and German, but also into Venezuelan indigenous languages, such as Wayú and Warao.

(28) What were the consequences of the "enabling laws"?

In November 2000, the National Assembly approved an "enabling law" (provided for in articles 203 and 236 of the constitution), that gave President Chávez special powers to legislate by decree on a wide range of issues related to social welfare and public interest. This power was granted to the president for exactly one year, or until November 2001. This "extraordinary" power, though not always called an enabling law, has actually been granted to almost all Venezuelan presidents since 1974. Indeed, throughout the region it is common practice to grant the executive branch legislative powers, as in the case of President Álvaro Uribe in Colombia, and former President Carlos Menem in Argentina, among many other recent examples.

The idea is that, while the National Assembly gets bogged down in partisan debates and infighting, the president has the temporary power to put key legislation into effect immediately. Thus, throughout much of 2001, President Chávez, with the support of special legislative work commissions, drafted forty-nine legislative decrees that he put into effect in November 2001, just as his enabling power was coming to an end.

One immediate effect of the promulgation of these laws was that the opposition was energized. They viewed these laws as dramatically increasing state intervention in the economy and in areas of individual rights. The laws addressed a wide range of issues, including regulation of the petroleum industry, land distribution, microfinance policy, and fishing rights. This response will briefly explain two of the most controversial laws; a third crucial law, the so-called Land Law, will be discussed in question 85.

The so-called Microfinance Law represented President Chávez's attempt to "democratize" access to financial credits by providing easy access and guaranteed low interest (in some cases as low as 1 percent per month, which is extremely low given Venezuela's inflationary tendencies) to vulnerable groups, including small businesses and women. This law also led to the creation of the world's first Women's Development Bank, and the microlending Bank of the Sovereign People, among other innovate lending institutions. Recently, the state has begun requiring that privately owned banks support the development of small companies, cooperatives, and small farms.

The Coasts, Fishery, and Aquaculture Law was conceived as a means of supporting small-scale artisan fishing communities. This law was widely debated because it undermined the tacit rights of the commercial fishing industry by declaring "public domain" all coastal areas that had not been legally acquired and limiting coastal fishing to traditional techniques. The opposition fiercely opposed the redistributive nature of this law, arguing that it violated private property rights and would undermine the national fishing industry. Four years after this law was implemented, the national fishing industry is alive and well, and coastal communities can freely engage in their traditional subsistence fishing. By pushing these boats into deeper waters, the law has reduced environmental damage from commercial fishing in shallow, sensitive coastal waters.

As these two examples illustrate, the enabling laws were based on the government's vision for social inclusion and economic redistribution. For their supporters, they represent major steps toward the implementation of the constitution's guarantees and the fulfillment of the government's socioeconomic program. For the opposition, these laws formed a central part of the context that led to the April 2002 coup.

(29) How did the new constitution change the political role of the military?

Although some Venezuelans continue to argue that members of the military should not participate directly in the political process, but rather maintain a neutral role, article 330 of the constitution has restored their right to participate in elections and in the democratic process.

In addition to the participation in elections expected from the implementation of this article, many dissident officers have cited article 350 of the constitution: "The people of Venezuela, true to their republican tradition and their struggle for independence, peace, and freedom, shall disown any regime, legislation, or authority that violates democratic values, principles, and guarantees or encroaches upon human rights." The role of the military has visibly changed since the implementation of the new constitution. Now, members of the military participate in the state's social programs, in areas such as urban renewal, food distribution, support for urban security forces, rural school construction, and international training programs.

The government has progressively incorporated more and more members of the military into extramilitary roles, finally putting into action a law that had been on the books since 1975. The military has come to play an active role in the political process, and many officers have stepped down from active duty to run for public office or to take leadership roles in state corporations or institutions. For example, the heads of the Ministries of Infrastructure, of the Interior and Justice, and of Tourism, and the governors of the states of Carabobo, Táchira, Falcón, and Bolívar, were all military officers. Some have criticized this trend as representing the militarization or "Castroization" of the government. Retired and active-duty military officers have held up to one-third of the positions in the presidential cabinet.

Large sectors of Venezuelan society (as the election of former military officers to several state governorships indicates) have supported this development as a way to bring in new political actors.

The participation of retired Venezuelan officers in the political process is hardly a new phenomenon; every government during the previous forty years of representative democracy included members of the military to one degree or another. What has changed is the state's willingness to use the armed forces to play a political and social role in the struggle against poverty.

Finally, President Chávez has terminated Venezuelan military-exchange programs with the U.S. military. Initially, Venezuela withdrew only its officers who were studying at the former School of the Americas in Fort Benning, Georgia, because of the history that school's graduates have of human rights abuses and illegal activities upon return to their home countries.

Eventually Chávez terminated all military-exchange programs with the United States because of what he described as U.S. efforts to turn Venezuelan officers against their government.

(30) What kind of government does the new constitution establish?

The new model provides citizens with the right to participate, evaluate, and even direct public policy. This model attempts to put the state at the service of the people. The new form of government is a participatory democracy, intended to stimulate people's participation beyond simply casting their ballots during elections.

Another characteristic of this new system of government that distinguishes it from the previous model is that political parties are no longer the sole administrators of state power. Local communities, civil society organizations, rural land committees, and cultural groups have come to play an active role in a wide range of state institutions and programs. In this way, the new model has attempted—not always successfully—to reduce clientelism by eliminating bureaucrats appointed simply because of party loyalty. The people have the constitutional right to participate, and through their involvement and direct observation of the government in action, they provide a unique kind of political pressure and oversight of politicians at every level.

Critics of the new system have a different analysis. For example, in *The Unraveling of Representative Democracy in Venezuela*, political scientists Jennifer McCoy and David Myers write that "the Fifth Republic Venezuela, when all is said and done, is less open and less pluralistic than its predecessor. Decision-making within it relies heavily on one person—President Hugo Chávez." José E. Molina, writing in the same volume, suggests:

> Deinstitutionalization and polarization in the party system, personalistic politics, and instability mean also that . . . the quality of Venezuelan democracy has eroded from where it was during the Punto Fijo regime. The decay of the political parties has not given way to a higher level of participatory democracy but to a period of severe instability in which democracy itself has been at risk.[8]

While it is certainly true that decision-making power within the government has been concentrated in the executive branch, that Venezuela has become deeply polarized, and that Chávez is a charismatic ("personalistic") leader, none of this in any way precludes the broader inclusion of the public at large—as the following chapter, together with that on the social programs and missions, will illustrate. The power of the executive branch is balanced to some extent by participatory measures as well as by normal checks and balances. This new relationship between the government and the people, in turn, opens the door to an entirely new form of democracy: unlike the representative democracies throughout the region, Venezuela is a *participatory* democracy.

Participatory Democracy

(31) What is participatory and "protagonistic" democracy?

Participatory and "protagonistic" democracy is a model that attempts to stimulate and guarantee the people's active participation in the process of governing the country. Today in Venezuela, this new model is being developed and promoted as an alternative to the more traditional representative democracy.

Participatory democracy demands that citizens play a role in developing government policy, prioritizing projects and budgets so as to benefit the entire community. It is a form of democracy that facilitates monitoring the government's progress and its level of corruption and inefficiency, and that gives the people access to all government institutions so that they can call for change where necessary. It is participatory because the people have a role that goes beyond simply casting ballots; it is protagonistic because the people play a visible role in managing their government.

The Bolivarian Constitution firmly establishes the people's right to participate in the democratic process. This mandate gives the people the political space to share responsibilities that had previously been reserved solely for government representatives. Representative democratic governments impede people's participation in prioritizing their problems, in distributing local budgets, in ratifying or revoking elected governments. For example, in July 2005, one of the authors visited a small Andean municipality in Merida State called Santos Marquina where the young mayor Balmore Otalor had organized a "participatory diagnostic," in which any and all members of the community were invited to participate. Some of the organizers of the diagnostic were assigned to take care of the children while others explained the process through which the community members would determine which problems were most pressing for them. Some sixty people, both young and old showed up for the meeting, which was held in someone's garage. The meeting covered issues such as alcoholism, the need for a new bridge to cross the river running down the middle of the municipality, and most pressing, according to the votes tallied, the lack of a regular supply of running water.

The next part of the meeting consisted of a discussion about what would be needed to solve the water problem, what the mayor's budget looked like and what the community could do itself without depending on the state or national government for help. The meeting, and others like it in Santos Marquina, will allow the municipality to set their 2006 budget with active participation from the town's residents in an open, inclusive and transparent manner.

Article 72 of the constitution indicates, "All magistrates and other offices filled by popular vote are subject to revocation." This gives the people the right to remove anyone from office who is not fulfilling the electorate's expectations, without the need to wait until the next election or for a congressional impeachment proceeding.

By becoming the driving force behind government policy, the electorate can also become the agents of change in their country. This model of democracy attempts to give life to the classic ideal of a government "of the people, by the people, and for the people."

(32) What are the impacts of participatory democracy?

One impact is that the opposition has the possibility to directly challenge the government in office by, among other things, initiating a recall referendum—which can divert the government's energy for months. Although this can be problematic for the government, the recall referendum also gives sectors of society that do not agree with the government a chance to demand redress for their grievances. It also permits, as was the case in 2004, the government to relegitimize its mandate. In sum, this process allows a society with political differences to reconcile those differences through peaceful, democratic participation. That an opposition can directly challenge the mandate of a government means that, although there will always be an opposition, the government's primary ally must be the community that elected it.

An example of the new alliances between the government and the people can be seen in the municipality of Caracas, where the community, through a local works committee, contributes to the mayor's office list of priorities and budget. This participatory process means that if a local government's budget is tight, the projects it undertakes will be the ones of most urgency to the community, not the ones that the mayor or his/her staff impose on the community because of other political pressures.

Another effect of this system of government is the community support that local governments earn by directly including the people. People defend governments that truly integrate them into the decision-making process, while rejecting those that continue to keep themselves separate. Moreover, the federal government provides financial incentives to stimulate participation: those governments that are most participatory actually receive more resources. Among these incentives are the Intergovernmental Fund for Decentralization (FIDES) and the Special Assignments Law for States (LAEE). The former obliges state and municipal governments to provide at least 20 percent of their budget to projects developed by communities and civil society groups. These funding mechanisms have led some to accuse the government of denying opposition-controlled governments their share of federal funding.[9]

Popular participation has helped to reduce clientelism and corruption in public institutions, since many high-ranking civil servants feel direct public pressure to perform. Another effect is the change of mentality within the bureaucracy of state institutions because of the greater contact between public servants and the public they serve. Examples of this change in public relations include the armed forces' new social-welfare role, and the responsibilities that state-run companies such as PDVSA, Cadafe, or the Venezuelan Guayana Corporation (CVG) have taken on (see question 38). Several of these companies have begun to operate under systems of worker comanagement and to dedicate some of their resources to social welfare programs, such as education or health missions (discussed in chapter V). Nonetheless, in many cases, the theory has not been put into practice, and corruption and abuse of public office continue to be serious problems in Venezuela.

(33) How have marginalized groups become active in the political process?

The Bolivarian Constitution seeks to eliminate social exclusion, and the societal violence that exclusion implies, by protecting the rights of minority groups and encouraging social programs that establish principles of fairness, access, and equity. Groups traditionally excluded, such as women, indigenous peoples, Venezuelans of African descent, homosexuals, the unemployed poor, and the displaced have begun to receive the political space to which they are entitled.

An example of this process of social inclusion is the advances of Venezuela's indigenous peoples. In no country in the world—even those where the indigenous peoples make up the majority of the population, such as Guatemala, Bolivia, or Peru—have indigenous peoples made so many tangible gains as in Venezuela, where they represent just 2 percent of the total population. The constitution recognizes that Venezuela is a multiethnic, multilingual, and multicultural society, and encourages indigenous groups to provide their children with education in their primary language, along with Spanish-language courses. These communities have the right to elect their own candidates from within their ranks based on internal leadership traditions. In Amazonas State, for example, which has a large indigenous population, an indigenous governor was elected, and there is significant representation of indigenous groups in the state and municipal legislative councils.

A much larger group that has also been historically excluded in Venezuela, people of African descent—who make up roughly 8 percent of the total population—has not been purposefully included the way indigenous peoples have been. Although as individuals and as families they can benefit from state services just as any other Venezuelan can, they have not benefited directly as a group as much as indigenous people, who now have an entire chapter of the constitution dedicated to their rights. Other excluded and marginalized Venezuelans, such as the mentally ill, do not enjoy better conditions or broader political rights than the mentally ill in other parts of the world.

The Venezuelan government has been able to facilitate a proactive role for the majority of Venezuelans, but for many, such as Venezuelans of African descent, this social inclusion is not achieved on a group-by-group basis, but rather through the general societal changes that impact all Venezuelans. The process of social inclusion has just begun. The government is still a long way from accomplishing its goals.

(34) What is the idea of one big middle class?

The idea that all of Venezuela can be one big middle class is a goal of President Chávez's efforts to end poverty. The lower class, the poor, have had no access to the basic benefits and securities of the middle class, such as education, housing, stable employment, internal tourism, and cultural consumption. The idea is to give the poor access to all of these things traditionally reserved for the middle and upper classes, thereby bringing the poor into the middle class.

In President Chávez's own words:

> One of my dreams is that Venezuela be a country with one big middle class, that we do away with extreme wealth and extreme poverty, that extreme wealth of those who acquire fortunes become exceptional. But, OK, they have a right to their riches, we are not going to take it from them, but if all of Venezuela could belong to the middle class, in the country and in the cities alike—a productive rural middle class of small-property owners, and an urban middle class; if only we could all have our own house, a job, a dignified and just income, to provide our children with high-quality and free education, health care, and sports.[10]

As Chávez indicates, this is not about attacking the wealthy or undermining the gains of the existing middle class, but rather about improving the quality of life for Venezuelans from the bottom up. This vision need not be rooted in class conflict, but rather in equitable development that eradicates poverty.

The majority of the government's efforts have been directed toward the poorest sectors of Venezuelan society. This has meant that key sectors of the middle class have often felt that they are cut out of the process, or that they are falling behind relative to the gains of the poor. This helps explain the separation between the middle class and the government that has grown steadily since Chávez's first election. Some analysts, such as Olga Dragnic, professor of social communication at the Central University of Venezuela, suggest that large parts of the middle class that voted for President Chávez in 1998 withdrew their support as they began to feel more and more alienated from his government.

The Venezuelan middle class was always one of the groups hardest hit by the country's inflationary tendencies—beginning with "Black Friday" in the 1983 financial crisis, when the government stopped propping up the national currency and sharp devaluation and inflation decimated their savings. Many in the middle classes had hoped that President Chávez would reestablish their historic buying power in the short term, something he most definitely did not accomplish, as he chose instead to focus his attention on structural reforms of the state system and on meeting the pressing needs of the country's poorest citizens.

The middle class is a diverse group, and some sectors continue to support the Bolivarian process. For example, most of the professionals and high-ranking members of the armed forces working for the government are part of the middle class and are dedicating their time, energy, and skills to the Bolivarian Revolution. Still, President Chávez is a long way from matching his popular support among the poor within the middle classes, much less from achieving his dream of one big middle class.

(35) How have women been affected by participatory democracy?

Women represent 49.6 percent of the population in Venezuela. The women's movement has been one of the strongest progressive movements in Venezuelan contemporary history and has won crucial advances for women and children over the past forty years.

The most significant changes in the Venezuelan legal code in recent years in terms of women and children were the 1999 Law on Violence against

Women and Families and the 2000 Organic Law for the Protection of Children and Adolescents. Further, the Law of Equal Opportunities for Women seeks to attack the roots of gender inequality: article 9, for example, obliges the Ministry of Education and Culture to "incorporate new teaching methods from preschool onward, oriented to modify sociocultural norms of the behavior of boys and girls." These laws represent the government's efforts to realize its constitutional obligations to a group that continues to be systematically excluded and oppressed in most of the world.

At the behest of the UN Population Fund, the NGO Sustainable Development and Population Network (*Red de Población y Desarrollo Sustentable*) wrote a report on women in Venezuela in which they included a list of women's gains in the Bolivarian Constitution, including article 88, quoted above in question 25; the gender-equal language; and the legal development of rights and responsibilities in marriages and civil unions.

Despite these legal gains, only 18 of the 165 National Assembly deputies (11 percent) are women. Only 2 out of 22 governors are women (9 percent) and only 20 out of a total of 335 mayors are women (6 percent). The majority of female representation is concentrated in the individual state legislative bodies. Women also play a leading role in the barrios, where they are the ones doing most of the political organizing, but receive all too little official recognition. Because of this explicit incongruity, the CNE passed a resolution in April 2005 that legally obliges all political parties to run an equal number of men and women. The newly created "Unified Command of Women for Unity and Parity" will process the complaints of excluded women and take their cases before the Supreme Court to ensure that their rights are upheld. State institutions like the National Institute of the Woman (INAMUJER) and civil society organizations like the Center for Women's Studies at the Central University of Venezuela are also playing central roles in defending women's rights.

Although there is a long way to go before women achieve truly equal political representation or equal rights in the workplace and at home, the new constitution, new national laws, and women's own initiatives in the political process have opened the door to huge gains.

Increased participation can be seen in the military, where women are now allowed to enlist. Although women were first allowed into the air force and the navy in 1978, the program was later suspended. President Chávez reopened it, and expanded it to all branches of the armed forces, so that there are no legal limitations on a woman's ability to build a career in the military.

(36) How has this model of democracy impacted crime, urban security, and people in Venezuelan jails and prisons?

The issue of urban insecurity is a structural problem dating back to Venezuela's shift from a rural agricultural society to an oil-dependent urban society during the first half of the twentieth century. Rapid, unplanned urbanization and the rise of urban unemployment made Caracas a dangerous place to live well before Chávez came onto the political scene. Nonetheless, under his leadership the problem of urban insecurity continues. Two primary factors can explain the revolution's failure to solve this fundamental issue. First, the structural causes of street crime, including unemployment, poverty, and overpopulation of urban barrios, have yet to be fully addressed. Second, the police forces throughout the country are still inefficient and corrupt.

A UNESCO report released on May 5, 2005, asserted that in Venezuela 22.15 people out of every 100,000 are murdered with guns—roughly equivalent to the rate in Rio de Janeiro.[11] In 2003 in Venezuela a person was murdered every 69 minutes, 9.6 people were raped every day, and 10 people were robbed every hour. Frustrated citizens regularly take justice into their own hands through vigilante mob action; on more than one occasion the authors have seen drug addicts, accused of stealing a purse or a cell phone, nearly bludgeoned to death while nearby police do little or nothing to intervene.

Venezuela does not have the death penalty, and the longest prison sentence permissible under the law is thirty years. Nonetheless, inmates in Venezuela's jails and prisons, most of them not yet convicted of any crime, have not benefited under the new government or from the participatory model of democracy. The horrendous conditions, overcrowding, violation of due process rights, and endemic violence that became commonplace in Venezuela's prisons well before Chávez took office have yet to even begin to change, despite the fact that Chávez himself served two years in prison after leading a failed coup attempt in 1992.

The country's thirty prisons have a capacity of fifteen thousand inmates but currently house just under twenty thousand—or 31 percent above capacity, according to the Ministry of the Interior and Justice. Of those twenty thousand inmates, less than 50 percent have been convicted and sentenced. A significant part of this overcrowding is related to a weak judicial system and prosecutorial inefficiencies. The government's justice system is simply incapable of guaranteeing due process rights. This deficiency has serious consequences for the country's inmates.

According to the Venezuelan human rights group Provea, roughly 300 inmates die violently each year because of unsafe conditions and overcrowding. In the first three months of 2005, approximately 110 prisoners were killed. Some prisons are reported to have an inmate-guard ratio of as much as 100:1. These same conditions make hunger strikes, violent protests, and prison rebellions commonplace.

Prisoners have constitutional rights to education, health care, due process, and so on, just as any Venezuelan does. Article 272 of the constitution specifically protects prisoners' rights: "The State guarantees a penitentiary system such as to ensure the rehabilitation of inmates and respect for their human rights. To this end, penitentiary establishments shall have areas for work, study, sports, and recreation, shall operate under the direction of professional penologists with academic credentials, and will be ruled by decentralized administration by state or municipal governments. . . ."

These constitutional guarantees have not made much difference in practice. The government has been unable or unwilling to provide basic security, nutritious meals, rehabilitative activities, or standard health care to the people confined in its prisons. Social inclusion or meaningful political participation in Venezuela's new democracy remains a distant dream for inmates, many of whom have already served more time awaiting trial then they would have faced upon conviction. Both a cause and a symptom of Venezuela's prison problems is the fact that the director of prisons has changed twelve times since President Chávez first took office.

In early June 2005, the Ministry of the Interior and Justice called a meeting with the directors of all thirty prisons in the country to discuss the grave problems facing the penal system. They decided to immediately begin introducing Mission Barrio Adentro (see question 42) health clinics in all of the prisons, and the educational missions as well.

(37) **How has this model of democracy impacted the opposition to the Chávez government?**

The opposition has engaged in outspoken criticism of the model, but has failed to engage the masses in the participatory process. Participatory democracy requires organizers and politicians to exert a new, greater effort to reach people. The people in the barrios and the countryside have come to participate directly in the political process, making it virtually impossible for a traditional politician to win votes without working in their communities, thereby proving themselves to their constituencies. It is no longer enough for a politician to pay for an aesthetically appealing publicity campaign or to appear regularly on TV as a means of garnering support. Opposition political parties have refused to accept the systematic changes brought about by the Bolivarian Revolution to the point that they often exclude themselves from the new model of popular participation.

During the five-plus years that the new constitution has been in force, a large portion of the opposition has focused its energy on undermining the new system of government and has refused to accept the changes already approved by the vast majority of Venezuelans. This focus has distracted much of the opposition from actually going into communities and organizing. In other words, instead of adapting to the new "rules of the game" and the new political context, the opposition has largely remained loyal to the old model. This loyalty to a system that once worked well for them, and their inability to adapt to the new one, has dramatically decreased their political popularity and, correspondingly, their influence at every level of government. Thus, sectors of the opposition have been described as erratic and without a clear strategy. Opposition political parties have practically abandoned public spaces, a fatal error in a participatory democracy. Some opposition leaders participate in electoral contests and public appearances only where there is ample media coverage.

One of the most innovative aspects of the new constitution is that it allows for any elected public official to be recalled through referendum. In early 2004, the opposition showed its ability to adapt when it began organizing a massive campaign to gather enough signatures to initiate the recall mechanisms against President Chávez. The opposition organized a widely based and extremely successful campaign that, together with international pressure, forced the government to hold a recall referendum. However, in the buildup to the referendum, the government's organizing base proved superior as it mobilized its supporters and won over 59 percent of the vote. Still, the fact that the opposition ticket won over 40 percent of the vote represented a significant development, a development President Chávez did not overlook. In the aftermath of the referendum, Chávez began speaking about how the government should be for all of the country, not just the majority that elected him, and he invited the opposition to play a more participatory role in post-electoral political processes. Shortly thereafter, the local and state election results showed that the opposition had not heeded his call.

(38) How has this model of democracy impacted state-run corporations?

Venezuela is currently in the midst of a historic debate over the role of workers in state-owned corporations. The state has largely trumpeted worker-government comanagement, while some radical sectors of organized labor have called for worker self-management both in cooperatives and in state-owned corporations. This debate was sparked in early 2005 when the government created the Ministry of Basic Industries, which is also responsible for the administration of the CVG, a group of state-owned companies that produce key raw materials such as aluminum, steel, electricity, and timber.

Along with this ministry, the government began a new policy of promoting worker comanagement, starting with the state-owned aluminum company, Alcasa. The Alcasa workers held elections to elect their own managers and foremen. This policy of worker inclusion in the decision-making process, especially in the election of the people charged with managing the company, has begun to spread throughout other state-owned corporations, especially once a newly comanaged Alcasa began breaking their old production records.

In the most powerful state-run electric company, Cadafe, the idea of comanagement actually developed even earlier, when both the workers and President Chávez witnessed the role the workers played during the December 2002 strike (see question 73) in retaking their factories and providing the country with desperately needed electricity—even as their management attempted to overthrow the government through lockouts and sabotage. Despite Cadafe's early start toward comanagement, in the first months of 2005 the Federation of Electric Workers' representative on the Cadafe board of directors protested publicly about the Ministry of Energy and Mines delays in moving toward full comanagement. The conflict led the ministry-controlled board of directors to fire managers who supported the workers' demands, though all those fired were eventually rehired after a successful worker campaign on their behalf. This case is particularly sensitive because of the national security implications of the electricity industry.

In general, the state has moved forward aggressively in guaranteeing that privately owned companies that generate substantial employment in important national industries do not go bankrupt. This does not mean multimillion-dollar bailouts as in so many other countries. Rather, when a privately owned company mismanages its assets or drives itself to bankruptcy, as in the case of the paper producer Venepal (now Invepal), or the National Valve Construction Company (now Inveval), the state has intervened to bring it under state control. In these cases, comanagement has become a central demand of the workers, whose chant has been heard across the country: without comanagement there is no revolution (*sin cogestión no hay revolución*).

This process has generated high expectations among Venezuelan workers in virtually every industry, including those in the private sector. Nonetheless, neither self-management nor comanagement has become the norm; rather, each remains an experimental model in a few state-run companies. Another issue yet to be resolved is the management model in the state's most powerful company, PDVSA. Just as in the case of Cadafe, during the December 2002 national strike, the workers—reinforced with manpower from the armed forces—were the key to regaining government control of this crucial state company, yet the state has been extremely reluctant to move toward comanagement within PDVSA. In this case it seems more likely that PDVSA will continue to be managed as in a state capitalist model, though perhaps the state will slowly give more power to the workers and allow for the rise of more cooperatives within PDVSA's ranks.

Workers in state-run companies have made historic gains in terms of worker control of the workplace and the means of production, even though this is a process that has barely begun. There are active debates within the labor movement and the government, which are certainly a crucial part of the process, but the many potential pitfalls and the high expectations about the future role of workers in state-run companies makes it impossible to predict the pace of development or the outcome.

(39) How has this model of democracy been received outside of Venezuela?

To begin to answer this question, one must remember that participatory democracy is an alternative to representative democracy, which is the dominant model in most democratic countries in the world today, including the United States. Although these two systems share a common democratic vision based on government power deriving from the consent of the governed, they represent distinct political philosophies that differ dramatically in their understanding of the rights and responsibilities of the citizen.

Organizations and governments outside of Venezuela that recognize the need to include groups that have been historically excluded in the political process have welcomed the idea of participatory democracy. Some social movements, in such countries as Bolivia and Ecuador, have incorporated the idea of participatory democracy into their demands and organizing methodology. Before the 2004 recall referendum, many opposition groups said that President Chávez was preventing the collection of signatures for the recall, and that this showed that it was not truly a participatory democracy.

Venezuela's experiment with democracy has led to a regional debate about democratic principles and ideals. For example, Venezuela requested that the OAS change its charter to recognize the strengths of participatory democracy, not just representative democracy. The relevant section of the charter currently reads: "Representative democracy is an indispensable condition for the stability, peace, and development of the region." Many countries accepted Venezuela's proposal to include participatory democracy, especially members of the Caribbean community, but the charter was not changed. Beyond major regional organizations like the OAS, Venezuela's efforts have become a point of reference for the poor, the excluded, the young, and the disillusioned throughout the region.

Some spokespeople of the Venezuelan opposition have asked the OAS to invoke its charter *against* the Venezuelan government, arguing that since participatory democracy is not stipulated in the charter, Venezuela is in violation of it, and is not a true democracy.

(40) What is innovative about this model of democracy?

Seen historically, the theory behind this model is not particularly innovative: it is simply the recognition that participation allows a democratic system to become more authentically democratic. In Venezuela, where an exclusionary two-party system defined the country's first forty years of democracy, the extension of democratic rights beyond simple participation in electoral contests has generated high expectations among the masses, and with those expectations broader and broader public interest and involvement in the political process.

In Venezuela, one thing that is definitely new about this model of democracy is that it makes widespread participation in the political process the rule rather than the exception. It allows all people—those disillusioned or excluded by the old political system as well as those who were active in it—to participate in the development of new political norms, which in turn makes politics a public activity rather than an elite privilege of public representatives or appointed bureaucrats. The change in the system of democracy can be felt in the streets, in the communities, in the barrios, and throughout civil society, where people have bypassed the traditional hierarchical, undemocratic party structure and formed participation networks, popular political or cultural organizations, and more. For example, the Seeds of Liberty (*Semillas Libertarias*) is a small cultural network in the barrio "Sector B" of La Vega, Caracas, that organizes members of the community for cultural projects, including a community-based radio station, puppet shows, documentary filmmaking, and a free neighborhood Internet café.

The new model implies and, if it is to be successful, even requires a change in mentality, an expansion of the political role and identity that Venezuelans have traditionally assumed. Now people are expected to actively participate, to assume responsibility at all levels for the healthy and productive functioning of their government. The idea of changing a deeply rooted political culture—the very mentality of the people—is not only an ambitious political goal, but also a controversial one.

This new participation involves grassroots action: helping set up government programs in local communities; sitting in on budget-allocation meetings; comanaging state-owned factories; creating local public planning councils that work with local government to develop public policy. Venezuela has also attempted to incorporate the experience of the left-wing governments in Porto Alegre, Brazil, that have innovated a model of participatory budgeting now being implemented throughout Venezuela, whereby local budgets are set by politicians together with community councils, including anyone from the community who cares to participate.

Perhaps what has stimulated participation more than anything else is the intense interest, energy, debate, controversy, and sometimes polarization that has defined Venezuelan politics since Chávez's election in 1998. Government supporters not only vote for candidates that work with President Chávez but also take to the streets to protest, and to organize. Finally, it is worth reiterating Chávez's constant call for the people to make the government institutions their own, to protest failures or abuses within the government, to pressure bureaucrats to produce, and to help detect and combat corruption through a range of avenues including participation in local diagnostic surveys and a social comptroller. Many groups that support the government have protested to demand the president's personal attention when the state bureaucracy gets bogged down. Thus, it is not uncommon to see pro-Chávez protesters in front of Miraflores Palace expressing their support for the government even as they demand immediate attention to their needs. The authors have seen dozens of these small, orderly gatherings featuring small farming cooperatives, workers in one of PDVSA's oil refineries, homemakers, and street vendors.

From the barrios to the factories, from the Presidential Palace of Miraflores to indigenous reserves, participatory democracy spans all levels of Venezuelan society and seeks to include every Venezuelan in the political process.

The Missions and Social Programs

(41) **What are the missions?**

The missions are extraordinary social campaigns through which the Venezuelan government is attempting to address its citizens' most pressing needs. The government developed the missions in an attempt to enact participatory democracy on the ground in order to accomplish campaign promises in areas such as health, education, food, housing, and employment, without reliance on the flattening and corrupting institutions and influences of bureaucracy.

The idea of the missions, as the name implies, derives loosely from Christian theology. President Chávez is a practicing Christian and has invited government leaders, members of the church, health-care workers, business leaders, and people from around the country to participate in helping Venezuela's most downtrodden in the tradition of Christian missionaries—following the example of Christ. For President Chávez, Mission Christ is the mission of the missions—a project to combat poverty, to strengthen the spirit, to eradicate hunger and the causes of suffering for the majority of Venezuelans. Mission Christ is a strategy, a platform of social projects whose ultimate goal is zero poverty in Venezuela. Chávez views Jesus Christ as the first socialist.

The impact of the missions, unlike most other government programs or macroeconomic reforms, is highly visible. While people may not understand how inflation and foreign currency reserves impact their purchasing power, anyone can appreciate what it would be like for someone who is illiterate to hear a knock on their door and get invited to attend their first class, right in their own neighborhood, and to receive a small government stipend to ensure they do not abandon their course of study due to lack of resources. As one grandmother living in the barrio known as Alianza in San Cristóbal, Táchira State, put it: "Chávez is the first president who even knows we are here. Our houses are still tin and cardboard, but now my grandchildren receive two meals a day in school. When times get really tough there is a Bolivarian Cafeteria up the hill, and there are several doctors living within walking distance who will see us and give us medicines for free." Beyond simply meeting the material demands of downtrodden Venezuelans, the purpose of the missions includes increasing the self-esteem and confidence of the poor.

(42) What are the successes and failures of the Mission Barrio Adentro ("In the Neighborhood")?

Barrio Adentro, as its name implies, is a mission based in the barrios where the poorest Venezuelans live. Essentially, it is a massive public health plan whose goal is to provide primary medical care in areas that previously had little or no access to even the most rudimentary medical services. It offers twenty-four-hour-a-day medical attention—including consultations and medicines at no cost to the patients. This social program is an attempt to provide for the sectors of society that have historically been excluded by a public health-care system that gradually deteriorated for all but the rich.

The mission of Mission Barrio Adentro is to build stronger, healthier communities through free, preventative health care for all Venezuelans. One of the means to that end is that doctors, dentists, and the rest of the medical staff move into the neighborhoods where they work and form part of the community, living and interacting with their patients on a daily basis. This mission works around the idea of preventative health care, which is developed in the context of the environments in which poor Venezuelans actually live and with an emphasis on education, sports, culture, and social security.

This mission was founded on April 16, 2003, with fifty-eight Cuban doctors, and has since extended to the whole country. Some twenty thousand Cuban and Venezuelan doctors, dentists, and sports trainers attend to the health needs of nearly seventeen million Venezuelans—or approximately 70 percent of the country's population—at no direct cost to the patients. From its inception through first quarter 2005, Barrio Adentro had registered more than 148 million consultations. Each doctor in the program has over 100 different medicines at his or her disposal for the most common ailments and diseases. Each doctor attends a daily average of twenty patients, and each dentist, just over eleven patients per day. All in all, Mission Barrio Adentro receives roughly two million visits per week and has an annual operating budget of $5 billion.

The government recently began developing Mission Barrio Adentro II, which extends the free health care beyond primary care to include specialized procedures. The initial clinics set up under this second phase of Barrio Adentro have X-ray facilities, ultrasound, optometry clinics, intensive-care centers, and more. The government is 40 percent of the way to meeting its goal of six hundred comprehensive diagnostic centers and an equal number of rehabilitation centers, along with thirty-three high-tech clinics. Barrio Adentro II is intended to provide the best medical care, on a par with Venezuela's top private clinics, for free.

Although the program is wildly popular, many Venezuelans have criticisms of it. They complain that the program is "Cubanizing" Venezuela, because most of the program's medical professionals are Cuban nationals. Some young medical students complain that it is taking jobs away from Venezuelans, though the Venezuelan doctors and dentists who share the program's vision for free universal health care have all been offered jobs in the mission.

Finally, the government has begun offering a medical degree known as "community health" that is intended to train a new generation of Venezuelan doctors who will begin replacing the Cuban doctors in the barrios. More and more Venezuelan doctors are working in the missions, and the first class of Venezuelan community health doctors will graduate from the UBV in 2007.

(43) What are the Bolivarian Schools?

The Bolivarian Schools are the educational component of the government's social justice campaign. The Bolivarian Revolution and President Chávez have slowed the process of privatizing public schools, prohibited charging matriculation fees, begun an antihunger program for students, and increased the national education budget from 2.8 to 7 percent of GDP.

The creation of the Bolivarian Schools began well before the first of the educational missions was founded. The goal was not only to build new schoolhouses throughout the country, but also to create a new educational system for students from the first through the sixth grades.

Although the previous constitution guaranteed free primary, secondary, and university education, by the late 1990s the state educational system had all but collapsed. In the wake of the widespread failure of the public education system, hundreds of private schools that benefited from state subsidies were founded. Through these subsidies, the state stimulated the growth of a private education system that failed to meet state requirements and that robbed much-needed resources from the state system. Despite the fact that state schools were officially free, they began charging a series of fees and often left the communities and families to provide all of their children's school supplies.

The Bolivarian Schools were born as the government began building schools based on a new vision for public education. Under President Chávez, the new government committed itself to making public schools truly free. As the schools are built, there is a focus on improving the physical space as a prerequisite for quality education, and on improving the conditions for education —including guaranteeing all students' basic supplies, uniforms, breakfasts, lunches, and snacks. In poor families where the lack of resources to pay for matriculation fees, uniforms, supplies, transportation, and food had often led students to abandon their studies, these changes greatly extend educational opportunities and serve as incentives to keep kids in school.

The impact of the Bolivarian Schools has been so great that thousands of older public schools—and even a few private schools—have incorporated themselves into the Bolivarian education system. According to a November 2004 report from the Ministry of Education and Culture, *Bolivarian Schools: Qualitative Gains of the Project*, the goal is to convert all public schools into Bolivarian Schools to improve and standardize the quality of primary education across the country. Nonetheless, the process of founding new Bolivarian Schools has slowed dramatically since the project's inauguration, and critics argue that many schools change their name to incorporate the word "Bolivarian" while changing nothing else.

By the end of 2004, nearly nine thousand Bolivarian Schools had been founded. According to information from the Ministry of Education and Culture, the dropout rate in Bolivarian Schools is a low 0.6 percent as compared to 4.3 percent in the old public school system. As a result of the elimination of enrollment fees in public schools, average enrollment increased from 59 percent in 1998 to over 67 percent in 2002—these are indicators of what the government's public education policy hopes to accomplish.

(44) What are the educational missions (Robinson, Ribas, Sucre, Simoncito . . .)?

The educational missions were developed through the Ministry of Education and Culture, with financing and logistical support from a range of state-owned companies and other ministries. These missions represent a key part of the Venezuelan government's broader policy of social inclusion and participatory democracy. Illiteracy and lack of access to education at every level exemplify the enormous social divide in Venezuela.

Mission Robinson was founded in July 2003 to combat illiteracy, which had hovered at around 6 percent, or 1.5 million adults. More than 2 million adults had never finished primary school; these numbers are extremely high for a country with Venezuela's resources. From 1988 to 1998 the Ministry of Education and Culture, private organizations, and Catholic charities initiated literacy campaigns, but their combined efforts yielded unimpressive results: just 73,000 Venezuelan adults learned to read and write. In its first two months alone, Mission Robinson enrolled 100,000 students. As word of the mission spread, it continued to grow, so that by April 2005, 1,406,000 Venezuelans had learned to read and write; on October 28, 2005, the government declared Venezuela "illiteracy free." Mission Robinson was so popular that the government decided to open Mission Robinson II so that graduates of the original literacy mission could go on to finish their primary education through the sixth grade. The government also founded Mission Ribas for all those Venezuelans who had yet to receive their high school diploma, no matter how old they were. More than 800,000 participants are working toward finishing high school in this mission.

Mission Sucre provides for postsecondary studies for those who never had access to universities due to space limitations, lack of resources, or the closed, exclusionary admission policies of most Venezuelan universities. In 2003 and 2004, this mission, which includes the newly founded UBV, with campuses throughout the country, enrolled some 100,000 new students. On the other end of the educational spectrum, Plan Simoncito supports preschool education and day care.

This series of educational missions is intended to provide ad hoc responses to the particular educational needs of Venezuelans, no matter their educational background. The higher-level missions often serve graduates of the lower ones, so that there are actually some people who set out to overcome their illiteracy through Mission Robinson I, went on to finish their primary education with Mission Robinson II, are now earning their high school equivalency through Mission Ribas, and are hoping to enroll in Mission Sucre. Students enrolled in the educational missions who require government support for their studies are given monthly stipends of roughly $100 to enable them to complete their education.

Although President Chávez promised to launch a postgraduate educational mission, this has yet to occur. In spite of enormous state support, the UBV has had serious problems getting started and has faced harsh criticism even from within its ranks. In early 2005 a large portion of the faculty quit, and Chávez fired the board of directors because of their failure to agree on a coherent curriculum. The remaining members have continued basic university functions and classes are still being held. In general, the educational missions have been criticized for prioritizing the quantity of students enrolled over quality of education provided. Some government spokespeople, such as Héctor Navarro, former head of the Ministry of Higher Education, respond that Venezuela's exclusionary educational system had built up a longstanding social debt, and that it is more important to guarantee equal access to education than to create a new educated elite.

Some 40 percent of the Venezuelan population, or close to ten million people—including three million in the missions—are currently enrolled in some form of education.

(45) What is Mission Habitat?

In Venezuela, especially in Caracas, substandard housing is a serious problem that impacts not only the poor and excluded, but also professionals and members of the middle class who have a stable monthly income. The statistics are telling: Venezuela lacks an estimated 1,600,000 needed housing units, and some 900,000 existing units have been condemned. Most of the condemned housing units are shantytowns known as *ranchos*.

Lack of housing is a dramatic indication of poverty because it destroys the social fabric vital to any community or family. To begin to combat the problem, the government put forward a housing mission, Mission Habitat, that includes a series of plans to address the paucity of housing. The most general of these plans was the creation of the Ministry of Habitat and Housing, which coordinates all of the state's housing policies and projects. The philosophy of the ministry, as well as the mission, goes beyond creating new housing units to consider overall community development as indicated in article 82 of the constitution.[12] The idea is that the government must support the creation of a safe, stable environment for all Venezuelans and eliminate dangerous, isolated *ranchos* that have no access to basic public services such as water, covered sewage pipes, or electricity.

More specifically, the housing mission began a new credit policy in 2005 that provides a huge support to the middle class. This policy lowers basic commercial mortgage rates from 17.5 to 11.34 percent and provides a one-time-only down-payment subsidy of nearly $9,000 for lower-middle-class families that earn less than that same amount annually. At the same time, the government launched a low-income construction program, prioritizing homeless families with children and communities that organized themselves into construction teams. Depending on the particular case, these groups have also been supported through subsidies such as free down payments, no monthly fees for the first several years, and a thirty-year timeline to pay off their mortgages with low interest rates. The urban land reform in progress (see question 84) is not officially part of the mission, but should help alleviate housing strain in major cities.

Government spokespeople have recognized the difficulties facing this mission due to the massive housing shortages in Venezuela. An estimated 130,000 new people enter the housing market each year. Thus the ministry has set a fifteen-year timeline for the development of its housing plan. Drawing on PDVSA profits and other sources of income, the government has guaranteed at least $1 billion to support its housing plans. Nonetheless, as of the summer of 2005, the government had made little substantial progress in reducing or improving the *ranchos* in major cities around the country.

(46) **What is Mission Vuelvan Caras?**

This mission, founded on January 18, 2004, was designed to fight unemployment, and thus, more generally, poverty. It also forms the grassroots part of the government's endogenous development program (see question 83). The name Vuelvan Caras (About Face) comes from one of the most significant victories in the war for liberation from Spain during the early 1800s. In the battle of Queseras del Medio, General José Antonio Páez used the battle cry *"Vuelvan caras"* to rally his 140 retreating cavalry to face and eventually defeat some 1,200 Spanish troops. Today, the idea behind Mission Vuelvan Caras is to rally the unemployed to face their difficulties and go back to work, especially in areas that support Venezuela's endogenous development.

This mission is a key component of Venezuela's endogenous development, based on the country's capabilities and needs. It has led the government to create a map of endogenous nuclei focusing on the following six areas: agriculture, industry, tourism, infrastructure, services, and strategic government industries. This mission provides support and training for millions of Venezuelans in a range of service and production jobs, with an emphasis on the development of cooperatives. New cooperatives are supported with "cavalry" grants as they get off the ground and ideally go on to form self-sufficient parts of a market economy. The government has already authorized more than 315,000 grants for participants in this mission.

Mission Vuelvan Caras is thus a sort of school for technical training and the development of cooperatives. The mission gives cooperatives preferential credit ratings and priority for state contracts, both of which significantly enhance their ability to compete in a market economy. On March 31, 2005, some 286,000 Venezuelans, organized into more than seven thousand cooperatives, graduated as the mission's first class. The state continues to work with these cooperatives to integrate them into endogenous nuclei for strategic development. The next class in Mission Vuelvan Caras is expected to have over a million members.

(47) **What is Mission Mercal?**

Mission Mercal is dedicated to addressing another of the most basic and pressing problems facing Venezuela's poor: hunger. The broader strategic objective of this mission is national food security. Food security means that the Venezuelan government wants to guarantee its population sovereignty and avoid dependence on food imports.

This external dependence had serious consequences during the December 2002 oil strike. At that time the multinational companies responsible for Venezuela's main food imports participated in the blockade, severely limiting the state's ability to respond to the massive food shortages. As its organizers intended, the blockade created a national security crisis as several major companies locked their workers out, bringing food distribution and circulation to a halt.

The events of December 2002, together with the earlier strike leading up to the April 2002 coup, were key factors motivating the development of the government's food-security doctrine, of which Mission Mercal is a core component. The mission began as government-supported, military-operated, open-air markets on major avenues in Caracas. In these markets, prices were controlled as a way to combat the strike's economic sabotage and the damage food speculators wreaked on consumers. The success of these markets led to the creation of a national network of smaller storage depots and distribution centers in populous areas. Demand for the products offered in these markets immediately surpassed supply.

Mission Mercal supports domestic food production but primarily focuses on maintaining an affordable supply for consumers. The first phase of the mission in 2004 focused on constructing 4,052 distribution centers and provided food to ten million Venezuelans, or 40 percent of the country. There are now over 13,261 distribution centers that have combined average daily sales of over $2 million, or nearly half of all food sold in the country. In addition to providing a reliable, affordable food source, these state-run markets provide discounts of up to 50 percent off the market price for some basic food products in a measure meant to protect the country's poorest from malnutrition. According to the Ministry of Nutrition, the discounts in Mission Mercal average 28 percent on products that have prices regulated by the government and 40 percent on unregulated products. To ensure access to the widest group of Venezuelans, there are now mobile markets in trucks, small neighborhood markets, and supermarkets located in densely populated urban areas. Together with these markets, the mission has presided over the rise of free nutrition centers, widely known as Bolivarian Cafeterias (*Casas de*

Alimentación, or *Comedores Bolivarianos*) that serve balanced meals to approximately 600,000 Venezuelans living in extreme poverty every day.

While many of the products offered in Mercal are also commercial and can be found anywhere in the world, the government has developed its own line of basic foodstuffs such as rice, beans, lentils, sugar, powdered milk, cooking oil, and so on. The packaging used on the government's line of foods is not designed to attract the consumer's eye or to sell more products, but rather to inform the average citizen of their rights and responsibilities; each package includes quotes from the constitution, with practical explanations in the form of comics.

The food products provided through Mission Mercal have overreached their intended market, and now people from all social classes are known to shop in these markets. As one member of Venezuela's elite—whose family participated behind the scenes in supporting the 2002 coup—confessed, "I just love the butter and the milk sold in Mission Mercal, so I always send the maid to buy those products there and do the rest of our shopping in the regular supermarket."

(48) What is Mission Guaicaipuro?

Guaicaipuro is the name of the indigenous cacique who led the resistance to Spanish colonization. President Chávez paid homage to this leader with the symbolic action of moving his remains to the National Pantheon, where Simón Bolívar and other national heroes are entombed. Mission Guaicaipuro was founded on October 12, 2003, the National Day of Indigenous Resistance, with the goal of redressing some of the wrongs institutionalized through the theft of indigenous land and the enslavement of native peoples beginning under the Spanish colonial government. The mission may play an important role in the government's efforts to fulfill its constitutional obligations to provide indigenous peoples with equal rights in a multiethnic and multicultural society.

Venezuela has a population of approximately 500,000 indigenous people, and it is one of the most impoverished, marginalized groups in the country. In light of the wide range of problems facing indigenous peoples, Mission Guaicaipuro combines the activities of all the other missions and focuses their services in indigenous communities. According to Minister of the

Environment and Natural Resources Jacqueline Faría, leader of the presidential commission on Mission Guaicaipuro, one of its primary goals is to survey and title indigenous land. Depending on the particular traditions and needs of the community, the land titles are collective, community titles, rather than individual.

The new model of society created in the Bolivarian Constitution respects the rights of indigenous peoples to their own political, social, economic, and cultural organizations, as well as their own religions and languages, and sovereign domain over their ancestral lands. This mission supports indigenous people's ecologically conscious development efforts in light of their harmonious existence within their habitats and the constant threat of extinction of their cultures. It also assists them in accessing their state benefits and their equal rights to participation in the economy and local and national politics.

(49) What is Mission Miranda?

Mission Miranda is named after Francisco de Miranda, a Venezuelan who fought in both the French and American revolutions and then came back to Latin America to fight for independence from Spain. The mission is a part of the Venezuelan military reserves. In Venezuela, the military reserves are composed of inactive members of the military as well as people who were never part of the military but have signed up to form part of the reserves. Mission Miranda incorporates all these people into a training program that includes academic as well as physical training. The reserves are also assigned to work projects to support social programs and to defend national sovereignty.

Mission Miranda is representative of the efforts to bridge the civilian-military divide in accordance with the constitution, which stipulates that reservists should, among other responsibilities, contribute to civilian life through participation in social-development projects. The idea of creating new military reserves is about expanding the army and increasing the military's capacity to fulfill its new social welfare and economic responsibilities. Previously, reservists fulfilled their duties outside their home state, whereas now they continue to form part of their community as they work to develop it. While this obviously makes for a much healthier relationship between the military and the people, it has been criticized as an attempt to militarize the country from the municipal level up.

In order to dramatically increase the size of the reserves, the army has begun offering reservists salaries equivalent to the minimum wage. On *Aló Presidente* on May 3, 2005, President Chávez announced that he expected the reserves to reach 1.5 million members, while General Julio Quintero Viloria, in charge of the reserves, indicated that they may grow to more than 2 million members in the medium term.

(50) What are the primary failures and successes of the missions?

The missions have failed to get completely past the bureaucracy and corruption that bogs down so much of the government. Monthly stipends and microcredits are often not paid on time; seeds for agricultural cooperatives have germinated while delayed in transit. The missions have also been criticized for not having any external measures to guarantee the quality of the products and services that they provide and for a lack of transparency with respect to their costs and distribution of resources.

There have been some high-profile, specific failures within several missions. For example, the UBV has faced constant delays and setbacks. Despite the state's efforts to distribute products produced locally, Mission Mercal continues to distribute Pepsi and Polar drink products—even though these companies participated in the December 2002 food blockade. In these and other cases the very mission the state developed to move toward food independence has ended up depending on the same multinational companies and imports that created the problem of food dependency in the first place. Finally, some of the missions have done so little that virtually no one outside of the government has even heard of them.

An achievement of the missions is the integration of multiple state agencies and the mobilization of volunteers across the country to help meet the government's ambitious social goals. The missions have obligated the various departments within the state to work together to achieve ends that go beyond any conventional responsibilities. For example, PDVSA, the most powerful, wealthy, state-run company, has helped finance the most costly missions, including Barrio Adentro; the Institute for Cooperative Education, which was on the verge of declaring bankruptcy at the end of the Fourth Republic, has been revitalized and is now used to form cooperatives in collaboration with Mission Vuelvan Caras; Mission Mercal, together with the Ministry of Land and Agricultural Development, has taken significant steps toward meeting the government's food-security imperative.

Aside from the profound impact on the lives of tens of millions of Venezuelans, the primary success of the missions is political: the poorest sectors of Venezuelan society see that their needs are finally being recognized and addressed, and thus are committed to the government's project. The Chávez government made bold promises about social progress in areas such as education, housing, and health care, and it is through the missions that the government begins to live up to its obligations.

The fulfillment of these kinds of social promises has dramatically weakened the political opposition, but the political purpose and activity of the missions have led to some criticism. As experimental, newly created social projects, there is much room for improvement, but the opposition has failed to suggest viable alternatives for meeting the urgent needs of Venezuela's poor majority.

The profound impact of the missions can be seen in the barrios, in rural settlements, and across every sector of the working population. In this sense, a mission is worth more than a thousand words: outside criticism cannot change the minds of the millions of lives these projects touch. The missions played a decisive role in driving Chávez's public approval rating above 70 percent in May 2005, while the opposition has been left without public leadership.

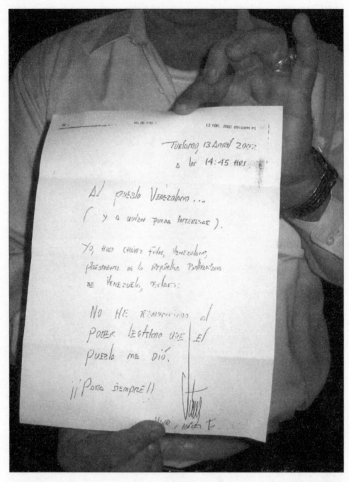

Letter from Chávez to the people of Venezuela while he was held at the Naval Base Turiamo during the 2002 coup denying the claims that he had resigned. *Courtesy of Presidential Press, Miraflores.*

April 14, 2002, Chávez arrives at Miraflores surrounded by loyal members of the military after being rescued from Orchid Island where he was held during the coup. *Courtesy of Presidential Press, Miraflores.*

The Metropolitan Police, under an opposition Mayor's control, repress a pro-Chávez protest during the coup. *Photo by José Clemente.*

One of the many protests against the government in upper-middle-class neighborhoods during 2002. *Photo by José Clemente.*

General Néstor González González was the military attache to the U.S. He returned to Venezuela the day before the April 11, 2002, coup. *Photo by José Clemente.*

The omnipresent El Libertador, Simón Bolívar. *Photo by José Clemente.*

Opposition protestors, holding rockets to shoot at the National Guard, choke on tear gas.
Photo by José Clemente.

One of Venezuela´s best-selling books, a common sight at protests. *Photo by José Clemente.*

Vigilantism in action: street vendors join up against a would-be thief. Caracas is still one of the most violent cities in the world. *Photo by José Clemente.*

Despite their ongoing poverty, the poor continue to support Chávez. *Photo by José Clemente.*

Political propaganda has taken a place alongside bikini models and sports heroes on the walls of Venezuela's poorest citizens' ranchos. *Photo by José Clemente.*

Pro-Chávez protestors regularly fill Avenue Bolívar in Caracas. *Photo by Wilmer Rumbos.*

The pro-Chávez faction of the National Assembly holds an open-air meeting when the Assembly itself is closed down by protests. *Photo by José Clemente.*

Chávez leads a Misión Robinson literacy class. *Courtesy of Presidential Press, Miraflores.*

The April 11, 2002, Coup

(51) **What happened on April 11 and 12, 2002?**

What actually happened on April 11 and 12 during the coup d'état that briefly removed President Chávez from office is still hotly contested. The hard-line opposition insists that there was a "vacuum of power" and not a coup d'état in the traditional sense. In this version, in the vacuum a new leader was needed, and Pedro Carmona answered the call of civil society by stepping up to the presidency. However, the evidence indicates that what occurred was indeed a calculated, conspiratorial coup whose complex plan began to develop when President Chávez was first elected and accelerated rapidly in 2000 and 2001.

Although the coup itself took place during just forty hours, a planned, highly coordinated general strike, organized with the support of the leading TV networks, the CTV, and the Fedecámaras set the plan in motion on April 9. Across the country, thousands of businesses closed in support of the general strike, and many—such as the Sambil shopping centers—went so far as to lock their workers out. A broad-based media campaign that presented the country as being on the verge of civil war supported the striking businesses. At this critical point, the country was polarized between those who wanted to support the Bolivarian project of the Chávez government and those who were trying to overthrow it.

April 11 began with a massive opposition rally that marched from the Altamira Plaza, a center for the opposition in an exclusive neighborhood of Caracas, to the PDVSA headquarters in Chuao. Once the marchers arrived, the organizers, in violation of the approved, publicized march plans, led the rally across the city to Miraflores, the presidential palace. Meanwhile, people living in the poor neighborhoods around Miraflores had begun to come down from their barrios, forming a counterprotest on the large avenues nearby. The tension was thick, and rumors of a coup began to fly.

The situation exploded with the gunshots of sharpshooters hidden in buildings near Miraflores. People in both groups fell wounded; the majority received lethal shots directly to their heads. The gunshots led to pandemonium. These sharpshooters, working with the metropolitan police in support of the coup, were attempting to draw fire from those carrying guns in the pro-Chávez march in order to manipulate the images in the media. They were successful. At least twelve people died and hundreds were wounded. Reports of the events on the privately owned television networks made sure that only members of the progovernment march were shown shooting, and newscasters indicated that the shootings had been on orders direct from President Chávez. These images and news reports—some of which were actually filmed before the events took place—were then used to trick loyal members of the military into withdrawing their support for the government, a key part of the coup plot. The trick worked, and President Chávez was left isolated from the vast body of troops loyal to him and the Bolivarian process.

Since earlier that morning, the military rebellion had already quietly begun, with unauthorized troop movements, blocking off of major arteries to the capital, and more. For example, a group under the command of the then governor of Miranda State, Enrique Mendoza, closed down the state-run TV channel, leaving the public wholly dependent for information on privately owned media conglomerates that were supporting the coup. When the president's security team activated Plan Eagle, an emergency security procedure, many high officials in the military refused to provide support, leaving the president alone with his personal security and a few troops that were in Miraflores at the time. That night a group of generals backing the coup gave President Chávez an ultimatum: turn yourself in as a prisoner or we will bomb Miraflores. There were still hundreds of thousands of people on the streets around Miraflores demonstrating their support for Chávez, and the palace was filled with civilians who work there offices. Leading members of the Catholic Church offered to serve as mediators so that the president would sign a statement of resignation.

President Chávez would only agree to resign on certain conditions. After the coup, he explained the conditions he stipulated the night of April 11:

> The first one was to respect the physical safety of all the people and the government. The second one: respect for the constitution, meaning that if I resigned I would have to do so before the National Assembly, and the vice president would have to assume the presidency of the republic until new elections were called. The third condition was that I be able to address the country live. The fourth one was that my cabinet and bodyguards be able to accompany me.

The rebel generals did not accept the conditions; they gave the president a deadline to turn himself in, threatening to begin bombing the palace if he did not cooperate. To avoid massive bloodshed, President Chávez turned himself in as a prisoner—but without stepping down as head of state. Those coordinating the coup, however, publicly confirmed Chávez's resignation.

In the early-morning hours of April 12, President Chávez was taken to Fort Tiuna and then to a military prison in the Turiamo naval base. Since conditions in the country were still unstable for the coup government, they held Chávez incommunicado on Orchid Island in the Caribbean. The plan was to either kill him or remove him from the country. Beginning on the morning of April 12, the national private media began a campaign announcing that the president had resigned, but replacing normal news coverage with cartoons, nature documentaries, and reruns of old shows. These canned programs were interrupted every once in a while to show officials from the Chávez government being arrested.

In the meantime, the coup's organizers were moving fast and had set up office in Miraflores. Shortly before 6 P.M., a swearing-in ceremony was hastily organized. Pedro Carmona Estanga, president of Fedecámaras, swore himself in as president of the republic as representatives of the silent backers of the coup—including the Venezuelan Chamber of Commerce, the managerial elite at PDVSA, the Catholic Church, the rebel military generals, the bankers, and certain foreign interests—applauded.

That same day, April 12, popular protests had begun throughout Caracas. The media ignored them, and also ignored police repression of the protests, though more people were killed and wounded on April 12 than on the day of the coup. And, behind the scenes, the new government was already persecuting high-ranking members of the Chávez administration, including the vice president and the president of the National Assembly—the two people who, according to the constitution, should have assumed national leadership in the absence of the president.

(52) Why was there a coup?

The economic and political elites that had run Venezuela for decades found themselves with no way to regain control of the country democratically. The development of a welfare state, together with a comprehensive agrarian-reform package and national control over Venezuela's oil industry, threatened the hegemony of Washington-supported neoliberal policies with an alternative model. Historically, any government in Latin America that has tried to deviate from the national and international status quo—as in the case of Arbenz in Guatemala in 1954, Allende in Chile in 1973, the Sandinistas in Nicaragua in the 1980s, and Castro in Cuba since the 1959 revolution—has quickly come under attack. The Chávez government was no exception.

From the local perspective, perhaps the most significant factor that led to the coup was the government's efforts to control PDVSA, a powerful state-within-a-state long accustomed to near-total independence from its owner. The Venezuelan government tried to make the management of the state-owned company consistent with its political vision, directly challenging local and global economic interests in the process. Although the opposition had been planning a coup for some time, it was President Chávez's replacement of the top management of PDVSA with people loyal to his government that sparked the events of April 11, 2002.

To fully understand why the coup occurred, one must also consider the Chávez government's entire political program, including the Land Law (see question 85), the Hydrocarbons Law, the Microfinance Law, and other radical reforms that impacted the nation's elite and their economic interests. It was this combination of reforms that led the opposition to attempt a coup.

From the global perspective, the coup was also intended to prevent the possibility of an alternative economic-political model; as the world's fifth-largest oil exporter, Venezuela was using its oil wealth and policy to gain political-economic autonomy. Under President Chávez, Venezuela has played a key role in relaunching the OPEC cartel and driving oil prices back up on the world market so as to finance domestic social programs (see question 78). Thus, this was also a coup against OPEC.

The motivations briefly laid out here are different from the rhetoric the plotters used to justify it. Ever since the 1998 election, the opposition had complained about the "authoritarian tendencies" of the government. They repeated the fear that Venezuela would become "another Cuba," and warned the world that President Chávez was leading the country toward a communist dictatorship. For many people within the opposition, the fear was real—albeit more because of the successful campaign of the opposition media than any objective conditions on the ground. Some even publicly stated that Chávez was an "idiot" and a "mulatto unfit to govern."

(53) Who was involved in the conspiracy?

No one will ever know all of the plans involved in the coup plot, and much of the planning and conspiring that made the coup possible has yet to be revealed. Still, the events of those forty hours indicate a great deal about who was involved and in what ways. The main conspirators can be divided, however messily, into five groups: political, economic, social, military, and international (see question 56). At the time, however, almost everyone involved played a political role, making it hard to neatly distinguish one set of actors from another.

Within the group most easily defined by its explicitly political nature are the representatives of the opposition political parties: AD, COPEI, and Primero Justicia (sometimes presented as independent). Members of these parties were responsible for the political planning behind the coup attempt. Their participation took a range of forms, including both political agitating and practical actions. Enrique Mendoza, for example, then governor of Miranda State and a member of COPEI, was in charge of taking control of the state TV channel. The police forces under the control of Alfredo Peña—mayor of greater Caracas and onetime confidant of Chávez—were implicated in organizing the sharpshooters that started the bloodshed on April 11. Enrique Capriles Radonsky—mayor of the Baruta district in Caracas for the opposition Primero Justicia Party—was among the group that laid siege to the Cuban embassy and persecuted members of President Chávez's cabinet. Other key players who had been anonymous decided to come out before the cameras after the initial success of their plot on April 11, including Luis Miquilena, ex-advisor to President Chávez and former head of the Ministry of the Interior and Justice.

In addition to these explicitly political coup plotters, there were also the social-economic opposition groups, including NGOs, civil society groups, and business associations. Of these, there were two main groups whose roles were decisive in bringing about the coup: CTV and Fedecámaras. Both of these groups were closely tied to the traditional dominant political parties. For example, the president and all of the secretariat of the CTV were members of AD. The Catholic group Opus Dei and its ties to COPEI led them to participate in Pedro Carmona's self-swearing-in ceremony on April 12, 2002. Fedecámaras was also one of the economic players supporting the coup, along with the leading private media companies, such as Venevisión, Radio Caracas TV, Globovisión, and the newspapers El Universal, El Nacional, El Nuevo País, and El Mundo.

The group of military officers supporting the coup included as many as eighty high-ranking officers, some of whom were close to President Chávez. One of them was General Manuel Rosendo, head of the joint chiefs of staff; another was General Efraín Vásquez Velasco, commander of the army; another was Vice-Admiral Héctor Ramírez Pérez, commander of the navy. According to Attorney General Isaías Rodríguez, Vice-Admiral Ramírez was responsible for organizing the military insurgents. General Guaicaipuro Lameda, then outgoing president of PDVSA, Admiral Carlos Molina Tamayo, and Generals Néstor González González and Enrique Medina Gómez all played significant roles in the coup plot as well.

(54) What was the role of the media?

During a press conference for foreign media held many months after the coup, on December 13, 2002, the representatives of the owners of Venezuela's leading private media openly declared their opposition to the Chávez government. These media moguls included Alberto Federico Ravell (Globovisión), Marcel Granier (RCTV Radio Caracas), Miguel Enrique Otero (the national newspapers *El Nacional* and *Así es la Noticia*) and Victor Ferreres (Venevisión). This press conference only revealed what had already been clear to viewers and readers for months.

Prior to the events of April 11, 2002, the media waged a campaign designed to energize the opposition and pave the way for the coup. A key part of this campaign, and a component that the international media picked up, was the idea that Chávez was fully responsible for the political polarization of Venezuelan society. The Venezuelan media also presented the government's oil deal with Cuba as the primary cause of the economic crisis (as opposed to the sabotage and national strike the opposition had organized), and strongly criticized most other areas of government policy as well. The collective weight of the TV, radio, and print news controlled by the opposition portrayed the government as a dictatorship and Chávez as a public enemy. The minute-by-minute coverage of the opposition strikes, protests, and marches, together with the manipulation of images and events, amounted to inciting the coup.

Were it not for this manipulation, particularly the coverage of the events of April 11, it is doubtful that the coup would have happened at all. After the opposition and progovernment marches converged on Miraflores, the media did not report on the assassinations inflicted by sharpshooters or the metropolitan police force. Instead, the media portrayed the dead as members of the opposition and reported that their deaths were at the hands of progovernment supporters firing on direct orders from Chávez. The news programs did this by looping narrow-angle images of individuals in the progovernment march shooting guns. The narrow angle cut out the part of the frame that showed they were shooting at members of the metropolitan police who had taken up strategic positions and were firing on the crowd, and the commentators presented the footage as though the shots were fired into the antigovernment march. As the carefully documented video investigation *Puente Llaguno: Claves de una Masacre* shows, using original footage and pictures, this was not the case.

At 3:45 P.M. on April 11, President Chávez addressed the nation via a *cadena*—an emergency national address that all broadcast media are required by law to air in full.[13] The private TV channels used a split screen to simultaneously show the president's speech and violent images from the streets implying that Chávez had a direct role in the violence. The minister of communication and information, Andrés Izarra, was at the time working as editor in chief of RCTV's El Observador news program. He explained that on April 11, the owners of the channel gave him a direct order to show "zero *Chavismo* on the screen." This internal censorship led him to protest and then to quit his job that same day. Still, the damage had been done and this manipulation played an important role in winning the noninterference of the majority of the military.

On April 12, the plotters believed they had already won. On a right-wing news program called *24 Hours*, the host, Napoleón Bravo, read a false statement in which President Chávez offered his resignation. He then interviewed Rear Admiral Carlos Molina Tamayo and Víctor Manuel García, director of the polling company Cifra, who was presented as a representative of civil society. Both guests spoke openly and frankly about the plans for the then successful coup, and both gave their thanks to "all of the private media" for their support in overthrowing President Chávez. Garcia revealed, among other things, that a few days earlier they had gone to Napoleón Bravo's house to film a canned news release where Hector Ramírez Pérez, surrounded by a group of high-ranking military officials, read a declaration of the air force's nonrecognition of the Chávez government. This video announced that six people had been killed in the area around the palace, even though it was filmed well before the shooting actually began.

(55) What were the interim government's first steps?

Throughout the entire process, the de facto government presented itself as a "democratic transition" government; however, its actions during its short reign indicate otherwise. Shortly after taking control of the state apparatus, the coup plotters broadcast live from Miraflores a ceremony in which Pedro Carmona swore himself in as the new president of Venezuela. In a curious incident, the organizers of the ceremony ordered that a six-foot-tall painting of Simón Bolívar be taken out of the room, supposedly to be burned, although some well-meaning employees hid it in the basement and it was later recovered.

After swearing himself in as president of the republic, Carmona issued a declaration in which, with one fell swoop, he did away with the better part of the elected officials in every branch of government, consolidating all of the state's powers under his personal control. The initial acts of this government included the following:

1. Changing the name of the country from "The Bolivarian Republic of Venezuela" to "The Republic of Venezuela";
2. Dissolving the National Assembly;
3. Removing "the Chief Justice and all the other justices on the Supreme Court, the Attorney General, the Comptroller General, the People's Defender and the members of the National Electoral Council"; and
4. Authorizing Carmona to remove any governor, mayor, or other regional elected officials from office.

After this initial declaration, the transition government declared that it would hold elections within a year. Their allies in Washington, Spain, and the international media continually repeated the announcement of the impending elections as proof that the government was truly "democratic." Meanwhile, the activity in the streets continued. The sharpshooters who were captured while Chávez was still in office were later released and have not been seen since. The metropolitan police of Caracas and segments of the army repressed the popular protests in support of President Chávez. In the time—less than two days—that the Carmona government was in power, at least thirty-eight leftist popular leaders were assassinated in Caracas.

(56) Was the United States involved?

There is no evidence that the United States participated directly in the coup. Nonetheless, there is extensive proof that the U.S. government had prior information about the coup, and that it supported the coup plotters and the interim government during its short life. The role the United States played amounts to foreign intervention.

During the first few months of 2002, several of the coup plotters—including Pedro Carmona, Isaac Pérez Recao, and Daniel Romero—visited Washington to meet with high-ranking officials in the State Department.

The Venezuelan military attaché to the United States, General Enrique Medina Gómez, returned to Venezuela the morning of April 11 to take a leading role in the military operations against the Chávez government. On April 12, after the coup had taken place, Ari Fleischer, then the White House spokesman, said:

> According to the best information available, the Chávez government suppressed peaceful demonstrations. Government supporters, on orders from the Chávez government, fired on unarmed, peaceful protestors, resulting in ten killed and one hundred wounded... The government also tried to prevent independent news media from reporting on these events. The results of these events are now that President Chávez has resigned the presidency. Before resigning, he dismissed the vice president and the cabinet, and a transitional civilian government has been installed. This government has promised early elections.

The State Department issued almost exactly the same statement at a press conference that day. Both the White House and the State Department talked about the developments of April 11 and 12 as though they were spontaneous events. Yet, these declarations, from the highest levels of the U.S. government, corroborate the version of events that had been planned in Washington with the coup plotters over the preceding months. Ample evidence that the U.S. government knew in advance what was going to occur and actively observed, if not participated, exists; for example, during the coup, the U.S. Navy sent an aircraft carrier into Venezuelan territorial waters, and U.S. Air Force planes violated Venezuelan airspace without permission. Moreover, according to both an *Últimas Noticias* news report published on April 23, 2002, and *Chávez Nuestro* (pg. 177, see suggestions for further reading) during the height of the coup, U.S. military officers Lieutenant Colonel James Rodgers and Colonel Ronald McCammon entered Fort Tiuna, where the Ministry of Defense and other high-ranking officers that supported the coup were based, and where President Chávez was initially taken as a prisoner. The figurehead of the coup, Pedro Carmona, later wrote in his memoir, *Mi testimonio ante la historia (My Testimony Before History)*, that he had met with the U.S. ambassador on several occasions and that immediately after the coup he met with both the U.S. and the Spanish ambassadors.

In 2005 the U.S.-Venezuelan lawyer Eva Golinger published a book titled *The Chávez Code* in which she follows the paper trail and presents a detailed, carefully documented description of the role the U.S. government played in the coup. The book includes nearly 100 pages of appendices of U.S. government documents, including financial documents and contracts that show definitively a U.S.-financed network propping up and promoting the opposition. Since 2001, the U.S. government has officially sent more than $20 million to opposition groups (unaffiliated with specific political parties) via the NED, the Office of Transition Initiatives (OTI), and United States Agency for International Development (USAID), among other government funding offices.

CIA documents declassified in 2004 clearly reveal that the U.S. government knew that the Venezuelan opposition was planning a coup. According to Congressman José Serrano (D-NY), some two hundred members of the Bush administration received copies of a document dated April 6, 2002, titled "Venezuela: Conditions Ripening for Coup Attempt." The document included the following passage:

> Dissident military factions, including some disgruntled senior officers and a group of radical junior officers, are stepping up efforts to organize a coup against President Chávez, possibly as early as this month, [CENSORED]. The level of detail in the reported plans—[CENSORED] targets Chávez and 10 other senior officers for arrest. . . . To provoke military action, the plotters may try to exploit unrest stemming from opposition demonstrations slated for later this month. . . .

These and other declassified documents are proof that the information the White House and the State Department propagated on April 12 was nothing more than the preplanned version of events and deliberate misinformation in support of the coup.

(57) Why did the coup fail?

The coup failed for a number of reasons, including the private media's lack of credibility; the authoritarian, antidemocratic decrees of the de facto government; the words of Attorney General Isaías Rodríguez broadcast live on national TV; and, most significantly, the millions of people who took to the streets and the support for President Chávez throughout the ranks of the military. This answer will briefly touch on each of these complex and multi-layered factors.

Not long after the coup, the armed forces mobilized against the generals who had led the coup to demand a return to the constitutional government. Of the approximately eighty top ranking officials who supported the coup plot, only two had direct command over troops. Virtually all of the other troops in the armed forces were under the command of officers who, after the initial confusion and misinformation, came out in support of Chávez. This reaction from the military can be understood in light of the fact that the vast majority of the people in the Venezuelan Armed Forces are from working-class backgrounds, and not from the elite classes that supported the coup. Obviously a coup of this nature cannot survive without the ongoing support of the military.

The actions of the short-lived Carmona government were excessively authoritarian. The Venezuelan people, with a forty-four-year tradition of democracy, albeit severely limited, had just overwhelmingly voted in favor of a new constitution. They were outraged when Carmona disbanded all of the branches of government, personally assumed their powers, and claimed a popular mandate to do so. Indeed, many people within the ranks of the opposition did not expect that their efforts to change the government would result in the rise of a dictatorship—precisely what they had come to fear was in store if President Chávez stayed in power.

These factors, together with the private media's inability to keep hiding the truth, made it impossible to continue maintaining a government set up à la *The Truman Show*. Attorney General Isaías Rodríguez's live appearance on national TV played a key role in helping undecided segments of the populace make up their minds and see through the untruths being propagated all around them. All of the private TV networks agreed to broadcast his address to the nation because he had promised to resign and to support the Carmona government. Instead, once the cameras started rolling, Rodríguez announced that there had been a coup, and that President Chávez had not resigned and was actually being held incommunicado. Although the TV networks cut off Rodríguez's message before he finished, enough information had been made public that tens of thousands more people took to the streets.

More than anything else, the coup failed because of the overwhelming popular support that the legitimate government continued to have, and because masses of people came out to defend their democracy. Millions of people across the country took to the streets in protest, demanding Chávez's release. After three years in office, Chávez continued to represent the best hope of the majority of the country that had traditionally been excluded from the benefits of the modern state and all those who had dreamed of real change. In Caracas, for example, hundreds of thousands of people came out of the barrios and surrounded Miraflores and various military bases chanting: "He hasn't resigned, he has been kidnapped!" "Soldier, with conscience, find your president!" And, "We want Chávez!"

(58) How was President Chávez rescued?

In the afternoon of April 13 in the city of Maracay, General Raúl Isaías Baduel and his brigade of paratroopers declared their support for President Chávez. General Baduel had organized the support of fourteen other generals, all of whom cosigned a declaration titled "Rescue National Dignity." The declaration, invoking the constitution and the laws of the republic, had five main objectives: (1) end the terror unleashed by armed groups violently defending the de facto government, (2) immediately restore the constitutional order, (3) avoid further violence, (4) force Pedro Carmona to step down, and (5) rescue the legitimate president and return him to Miraflores (although they did not explicitly state the last one).

The document quickly circulated throughout the city, strengthening people's demands for the return of President Chávez. That same night in Caracas, troops from the Honorary Presidential Guard, with support from the hundreds of thousands of people still in the streets around Miraflores, regained control of the palace. At 8:12 P.M. on April 13, the legitimate government transmitted a message to the country indicating its return to power. Some two hours later, the president of the National Assembly, William Lara, swore in then Vice President Diosdado Cabello—who had been in hiding because of the persecution of the Carmona government—as interim president, in accordance with the constitution. Carmona, his support evaporating before his eyes, quickly stepped down and recognized Cabello as interim president.

Meanwhile, General Baduel and other loyal officers had organized a division of helicopters with support from navy swift boats to rescue President Chávez, who was still being held on Orchid Island. They succeeded in their mission without having to fire a single shot; around 3 A.M. on April 14, President Chávez arrived at Miraflores to reclaim his office. When he arrived, the masses of people were still gathered around the palace, waiting to welcome him home.

(59) How did the world react to the coup?

The life of the Carmona government was so short that most countries did not have time to react through official diplomatic channels. Nonetheless, the actions of several countries, especially those in the region, but also including Spain, are telling.

The Bush administration used the coup as an opportunity to criticize the Chávez government but reserved any and all criticisms of Carmona and the coup plotters. In fact, according to a *New York Times* quote from an anonymous high-ranking member of the State Department's Western Hemisphere Division, Otto Reich, then assistant secretary of state for Western Hemisphere Affairs, had called Pedro Carmona on April 12 to discuss his first presidential decrees. The State Department later denied that this phone call had taken place. The same day, members of the Bush administration advised Congress that President Chávez had resigned, despite the fact that, as declassified CIA documents show, they had prior knowledge that he had in fact *not* resigned.

Spain also had prior knowledge of the coup plot and also failed to advise the Venezuelan government of the imminent danger. After the coup and the de facto government's first authoritarian decrees, the Spanish ambassador, Manuel Viturro, together with the U.S. ambassador, Charles Shapiro, met with Carmona.

Unlike the conciliatory positions that the United States and Spain adopted toward the Carmona government, the OAS, in an emergency meeting, condemned the interruption of democratic rule and the dissolution of the constitutional government, citing the Inter-American Democratic Charter. The presidents of Nicaragua, Argentina, Paraguay, and Panama declared the Carmona government illegitimate and refused to recognize it. Brazil condemned the coup and also invoked the Inter-American Democratic

Charter. The president of Chile called for early elections and a return to democracy. The president of Mexico indicated that his government would not recognize Carmona until he was elected democratically. President Francisco Flores of El Salvador was the only Latin American head of state who recognized Carmona as president of Venezuela.

(60) **What was the "constitutional coup"?**

One of the biggest problems in the wake of the April 2002 coup was widespread impunity. On April 14, 2002, President Chávez addressed the nation to say: "The first and most important thing I want to say is that you go back to your homes, that you leave the streets in peace. All you Venezuelans who oppose me, well, you have the right to oppose me, I hope to be able to win your support, but at least you must recognize the constitution, it is for all of us. . . . The opposition has the right to peaceful dissent. . . ." He told the nation that he did not "hold a grudge or bear any ill will toward anyone" and that there would "be no witch hunts and no retaliation. . . . We will analyze the causes calmly, to make right any wrongs, we will make the situation right and in the meantime, peace and order."

Few were willing to assume responsibility for what happened. In the debates that took place in the National Assembly, almost all of the representatives from opposition parties refused to recognize that there had been a military rebellion or even a coup d'état, arguing that there had been a "power vacuum." Those who had signed the Carmona decree said that they had been in Miraflores just as "observers" and that they were forced to sign. Even Carmona himself evaded taking any responsibility, arguing that he was just fulfilling the duty that sectors of the military and civil society called on him to fulfill. According to this logic, the kidnapping of the president, the dissolution of all of the branches of government, and the derogation of the constitution seem to be of secondary importance—and perhaps even justifiable. Carmona was held under house arrest but ultimately fled to Colombia, where he was given political asylum.

President Chávez's supporters began to call for a firm hand in dealing with the coup plotters and with those who had supported undermining the elected government. In his addresses to the nation, President Chávez responded that it was not within his power to judge or incarcerate, that there existed other branches of the government for that—particularly the attorney general and the Supreme Court.

The impunity reached its climax on August 14, 2002. A decision signed by eleven of the twenty members of the Supreme Court rejected the attorney general's case against four high-ranking military officers who had participated in the coup and were charged with military rebellion. The ruling freed them from any responsibility for the events from April 11 to April 14, during which time more than fifty people were killed, the constitutional government was dissolved, and countless acts of looting and random violence were perpetrated. In its decision, the court refused to even recognize that there had been a coup or a military rebellion, thus setting a precedent that made it nearly impossible to hold anyone legally accountable for the short-lived overthrow of the constitutional government. The ruling also derogated from earlier Venezuelan jurisprudence in which the Supreme Court had recognized previous acts of military rebellion— including events in the 1960s and the two coup attempts in 1992—sentencing participants in those rebellions to as much as thirty years in prison.

Attorney General Rodríguez called the Supreme Court's decision a political rather than a legal one. Ironically, the court that refused to recognize the coup was the same court that Carmona dissolved with one of his first acts of government.

The Media

(61) **What is happening with the media in Venezuela?**

Venezuela is in the midst of a media war. The private media regularly attacks the government, accusing it of trying to establish a dictatorship and eliminate freedom of speech. The government accuses the private media of seeking to destabilize and even overthrow the government. The media began its campaign against President Chávez during his 1998 presidential campaign, though at the time it manifested itself as tacit support for the opposition candidates.

Once President Chávez took office and it became clear that he would not represent the interests of Venezuela's economic elite nor give the media their traditional input into his cabinet appointments, the media campaign against his government intensified. Initially, the private media simply dedicated more and more space to opposition groups or parties, and to news and opinion shows that were highly critical of the government. In 2002, the media played a key role in making the April coup possible, and in supporting the subsequent national strike in December. The media has regularly and openly called for the overthrow of President Chávez and has been widely accused of inciting violence through manipulation of video footage and news information.

When the government has tried to respond to these attacks, it has been accused of violating freedom of speech rights or of being tyrannical. For example, when Tobías Carrero Nácar—the owner of a multinational insurance company—brought a lawsuit for defamation against Pablo López Ulacio—editor and director of the weekly paper *La Razón*—and the court ruled in favor of Carrero Nácar, many people blamed the result on Chávez, citing the case as evidence of the threat to freedom of speech. President Chávez's charismatic style of governing and of speaking, along with his regular use of *cadenas*, has only fueled the media campaign against him and his government. His threats to suspend broadcast rights were poorly thought out and extreme. The actions of each side must be understood in the context of a media war, of high-stakes national issues and economic interests.

(62) Who owns the leading private media?

The traditional newspapers in Venezuela were once family owned and operated, and some were even founded as part of the political struggle against the dictators who ruled Venezuela until 1958. Now almost all of the national newspapers are administrated by the next generation of the original families, who have become powerful economic groups—though, of course, many of them were already quite wealthy. Most of the major newspapers in Venezuela now have international alliances; for example, *El Nacional* and *El Universal* are allied with *Time* and *Fortune*, respectively.

Two primary groups control the magazine market in Venezuela: the Capriles chain and the Bloque de Armas. Between them they account for more than 50 percent of the market. In the 1990s, these groups sold over $70 million a year in advertising. Just like the aforementioned newspapers, both of these magazine distribution chains have major financial interests in other communications media and other sectors of the economy. The Capriles chain controls eleven companies in addition to its three newspapers and five magazines. The Bloque de Armas group owns thirteen companies in addition to its newspapers, seventeen magazines, and a TV transmitter.

The radio market has traditionally been tied to the two political parties, AD and COPEI. These two parties controlled all the branches of the government and were responsible for handing out rights to particular wavelengths. Although these parties are no longer in power, much of the radio market is controlled by their former leaders, or by economic groups with traditional ties to them. Economic groups with diversified interests beyond communications control roughly 75 percent of the radio transmitters in the country.

In addition to the political groups that control large sectors of the radio market, major economic groups have also made investments in this sector. For many years the rival Cisneros and Phelps groups owned the leading TV channels. This balance was upset in the early 1990s when the Cisneros group acquired a new channel, Televen, which was the only other VHF signal available for private broadcasting at the time. Concurrently, the Cisneros group established a chain of radio stations called Unión Radio, dedicated exclusively to news programming. The group 1BC, which owns the TV channel RCTV, also controls the radio station RCR.

In Venezuela, just as in the rest of Latin America and the United States, TV is the most influential communication media. The country has four national channels (three are private and one has become state-run) and more than twenty regional channels. The privately owned national channels import roughly 65 percent of their programming, primarily from the United States.

Since 2002, the government has made an effort to break the corporate control of radio transmitters through a series of investments in community-based transmitters, including the *Circuito Mundial* network, which the government was originally forced to acquire during the 1994 economic crisis, and RNV, which has both AM and FM stations. Thus, ministries and state governors such as the Ministry of Education and Culture and the governor of Guárico State have been able to develop public-interest programming.

(63) **Is it true that the media have "functioned like political parties"?**

During the last three governments of the so-called Fourth Republic, corruption and mismanagement led to the gradual collapse of state institutions and with them the dominant political parties, AD and COPEI. President Chávez's dramatic victory in the presidential election in 1998 left these two (now opposition) parties demoralized and displaced.

The interest groups that traditionally brushed shoulders with the

country's political leaders—the upper echelons of the Catholic Church, busi-
nessmen, and leaders of major economic groups—began to worry about the
lack of a counterbalance to Chávez in the wake of their representatives' dis-
placement. Faced with a paucity of opposition political leadership, many of
these groups began investing their hopes, energies, and resources in the corporate media.

Consequently, the media increasingly took on an active political role.
Given the laissez-faire approach to media regulation in place when President
Chávez was elected, the media had the legal space to begin an unprecedented political campaign, leaving behind any pretenses of being "fair and
balanced."

The opposition political parties quickly adapted to this reality. Rather
than trying to go into the communities, universities, and labor organizations
to organize constituencies, they began to seek invitations to appear on TV
shows. The secretary general of the AD party, Henry Ramos Allup, has said
as much; in an interview with El Universal he admitted that the party leadership had largely begun to follow their media contacts, who began calling
the shots. Thus, as the traditional political parties lost their political space,
the national media chains began to fill the void.

(64) How did the media operate under previous governments?

When Venezuela's Punto Fijo democracy began in 1958, the AD and COPEI
parties came to control not only the country's political institutions, but also a
large share of the media, through patronage and clientelism. During the forty
years of puntofijismo there were occasional disputes between the government
and media outlets, but these were exceptions to the rule, since the people controlling the government generally represented the economic interests of the
owners of the private media.

Even when one media outlet had trouble with the government, the
others stayed out of it rather than taking the all-for-one approach that has
become the norm during the Chávez administration. The daily newspaper El
Nacional is a good example: during Rómulo Betancourt's presidency
(1959–1964), the government, together with the National Publicity Association, cut off the newspaper's publicity because its owner and director,

Miguel Otero Silva, had taken an editorial line in support of the Cuban revolution, which the government saw as a dangerous precedent. Otero Silva ended up resigning and handing over editorial control to someone whose politics were closer to the views of the president and the interest groups supporting him.

During the government of Raúl Leoni (1964–1968), the press and the government worked together against guerrillas who were then using armed struggle to try to overthrow the government. Under Rafael Caldera's presidency (1969–1974), the only notable hostility between the government and the media involved Miguel Angel Capriles, owner of the Capriles media chain and then a member of the national congress. He was elected along with seven other congressmen from his region, all of whom were members of the COPEI party, as was President Caldera. Capriles was dissatisfied with Caldera's cabinet and used his newspapers to pressure the government to change its appointments. Despite his status as a senator and as a well-connected businessman, a military tribunal issued a warrant for his arrest. Rather than trying his luck with the justice system, Capriles took refuge in the Nicaraguan embassy and eventually went into exile in Panama.

The most serious confrontation between the government and the media prior to President Chávez's arrival on the political scene occurred during Luis Herrera Campíns' administration (1979–1984). Then president Herrera Campíns decreed a series of laws designed to regulate the telecommunications sector, including the elimination of cigarette and alcohol ads from radio programs. These laws earned the president the fiercest media offensive up to that point in Venezuela's history. The government of Jaime Lusinchi (1984–1989) was accused of trying to control the media through manipulation of currency-exchange markets and through offering preferential exchange rates to the media outlets that supported its political line.

The second government of Carlos Andrés Pérez (1989–1993) marked the definitive beginning of the neoliberal era in Venezuela, which the media (and its corporate ownership) widely applauded. As the "tighten your belts" part of the structural adjustments the president implemented led to widespread public dissatisfaction and even popular uprisings, some of the media moved away from its initial enthusiastic support. Some papers, like *El Nuevo País*, began to actively call for the resignation of the president. Nonetheless, in the most difficult moments of his presidency, like the *Caracazo* in February 1989 and the military uprisings in February and November 1992, Pérez counted on the support of the media. During Rafael Caldera's second term as president (1994–1999), there were no major conflicts between the government and the media.

(65) How has the government confronted its problems with the private media?

Since President Chávez took office, one of the primary criticisms from within his ranks has been that his government does not have a well-developed public relations policy. For the first several years of his administration, the only PR response that the government had to the opposition media campaign was the presidential *cadena*. In other words, the government's public image depended largely upon the charisma of the president and his skill in communicating with the nation. It was precisely with the intention of better exploiting his public relations skills and his connection to the people that Chávez developed the show *Aló Presidente*, in which he takes call-ins from citizens and which quickly became one of the most popular and influential shows on both radio and TV.

Despite the popularity of *Aló Presidente* and the value of the president's direct communication with the people, it is only one show, once a week, and could hardly be expected to match the nonstop onslaught of the opposition-controlled media. Moreover, the private media have always had better technology, more resources, and access to popular foreign programming. During the April 2002 coup, for example, the government was unable to respond to the media offensive with its deteriorated media outlets—then consisting of two national radio transmitters, one television channel, and a national newswire. The government's media handicap played a significant role in making the coup possible —it was largely media driven. In 2002, the state TV channel relied on just eight camera crews, while Globovisión, a regional news channel covering the capital region and one of the leaders of the media opposition, had thirty camera crews.

Faced with this massive handicap, the government decided to found the Ministry of Communication and Information in the aftermath of the failed 2002 coup. The state has also expanded its media outlets to include two TV channels, one of which (VTV) is now being extended to cover all of Venezuela's territory. The government is steadily increasing the number of state-run radio transmitters, and has expanded and renamed its newswire "the Bolivarian News Agency."

In terms of Venezuela's international media strategy, in April 2004 the government invested roughly $4 million in expanding its international shortwave radio broadcaster, National Radio of Venezuela, to reach all of the territory from Canada to Chile. President Chávez has also aggressively developed the idea of Telesur—a TV news channel modeled on Al Jazeera. Telesur is expected to become a regional news source that rivals CNN en Español and Univisión, the current leading regional news networks. The project has already won the support of Brazil, Argentina, and Uruguay, who have offered to supply news material, resources, and, most importantly, audiences. In May 2005, Telesur began to develop programming for its channel and to run test broadcasts. The channel will provide twenty-four-hour news coverage broadcast via satellite throughout Latin America beginning in July 2005. For its founders, Telesur represents the possibility of giving an alternative voice and vision to the people of Latin America, long accustomed to receiving their news from one of a few private networks. By the end of 2005, the channel hopes to have correspondents in Madrid, Bogotá, Buenos Aires, Brasilia, and Los Angeles. Also significant are Venezuela's plans to launch a Chinese-made satellite by the end of 2008.

(66) How has this government supported independent media?

Given that ownership of Venezuela's media outlets is highly concentrated and that 65 percent of all TV programming is imported from abroad, it should come as no surprise that average Venezuelans are not given space in most of the country's privately owned media.

The current government has argued for the need to "democratize" the media through the creation of new media outlets. The government has also supported a proactive role for citizens in analyzing, critiquing, and even creating news material. Specifically, the government has distributed TV cameras and radio broadcasters to community groups and has legalized a range of underground press and radio through a revision of the national radio and TV regulations, all to counterbalance the private chains. It expects to have distributed at least 128 local radio transmitters by the end of 2005.

The president has also encouraged the National Assembly to pass laws that stimulate citizen participation in the media from the grassroots up. To that end, it has funded more than three hundred training courses for community-based radio transmitters and opened the Latin American School for Documentaries to stimulate independent, in-depth news production. Along the same lines, material produced by members of the recently established National Registry of Independent Producers is reserved a minimum of 5.5 hours out of every 24 hours of programming on radio and TV media, so as to stimulate local arts, music, and media production.

On the user end, more than 250 "Radio and TV Consumer Committees" have been founded since November 2004. These groups have the responsibility to monitor the rights of their communities vis-à-vis state, private, and independent media. They also represent a practical way to include the grassroots in national debates about media regulation. William Castillo, vice minister of media management in the Ministry of Communication and Information, has said that these policies are intended to "incorporate new groups and producers that will stimulate the reorganization of the media to break the monopoly held by private interests."

(67) What are the primary criticisms of Venezuela with regard to freedom of expression and the press?

Many of the complaints with regard to freedom of speech are illogical and groundless, such as a headline in *El Universal* in November 2004 declaring that the media law being debated in the National Assembly would "end 110 years of freedom in Venezuela." Since Venezuela has had democratic governments only since 1958, the mention of 110 years of freedom is illogical at best.

During the coup attempt and the national strikes in 2002, pro-Chávez protestors attacked opposition journalists on dozens of occasions, and the government has been criticized for not doing more to protect journalists from physical assaults. Chávez also regularly uses *cadenas*, which interrupt regular programming and force every channel and station to carry his speeches live.

The government has carried out a series of investigations into the behavior of the leading private media channels, including tax audits and the application of rarely enforced articles of communications laws. The opposition argues that these investigations and enforcements are politically motivated, and that the harsh sanctions for noncompliance with communications regulations are intended to create a climate of "self-censorship." The government has also passed a series of new laws that give it increasing control over private media. For example, in March 2005, the government approved a series of amendments to the criminal code that extend the scope of existing provisions making it a criminal offense to insult or show disrespect for the president and other government authorities, and that increase the penalty for libel and public defamation to up to four years in prison and steep fines. One of the most controversial steps the government has taken in the media war has been to pass the Social Responsibility in Radio and Television Law.

(68) What is the "gag law" or the Social Responsibility in Radio and Television Law?

The "gag law" is the name the opposition and the private media have given to the law officially known as the Social Responsibility in Radio and Television Law, which the National Assembly passed in November 2004. The stated purpose of the law is to define and:

> Establish the social responsibility of radio and television service providers, related parties, national independent producers, and users in the process of broadcasting and reception of messages, promoting a democratic equilibrium between their duties, rights, and interests, with the goal of seeking social justice and contributing to citizenship formation, democracy, peace, human rights, education, culture, public health, and the social and economic development of the Nation, in conformity with constitutional norms and principles, legislation for the holistic protection of boys, girls, and adolescents, education, social security, free competition, and the Organic Telecommunications Law.

The opposition often describes the law as heralding the end of the democratic system and the imposition of tyranny in Venezuela.

The law provides a series of comprehensive—but often vaguely worded—regulations on radio and television broadcasting rights. The full text of the law can be purchased for $2 on street corners throughout the country. Its function is broadly comparable to that of legislation in the United States such as the Communications Decency Act of 1995. Certain clauses in the Venezuelan legislation have become extremely controversial; for example, the law has been criticized for having loosely worded rules on incitement of breaches of public order that could penalize broadcasters' legitimate expression of political views. If found responsible for the infractions, a television or radio station could be ordered to suspend transmissions for up to seventy-two hours and have its broadcasting license revoked upon a second offense. The owners and editorial boards at leading private media channels argue that these provisions force them to self-censor to avoid falling into gray areas and facing stiff penalties.

The law favors national artists, musicians, and independent media groups, but at the expense of editorial flexibility. For example, all media outlets are required to program as much as 40 percent of their airtime with media content from independent producers. Radio stations are now required to play at least one Venezuelan song for every foreign song played.

The law also establishes an eleven-person Directorate of Social Responsibility, which is comparable to the five-person Federal Communications Commission (FCC) in the United States. Its president, the director general of the National Telecommunications Commission (CONATEL), is appointed by the president of the republic. The other members include one representative from each of the ministries of Communication and Information, Education and Culture, and Health, and one representative each from the National Women's Institute, the National Council for Children and Adolescent Rights, the religious sector, academia, NGOs dealing with the protection of children and adolescents, and two representatives from user organizations. The latter four representatives are selected in an assembly convoked by CONATEL. The directorate's duties include (1) to discuss and approve technical norms derived from the law, (2) to establish and impose sanctions not assigned to CONATEL's director or the Ministry of Infrastructure, and (3) to manage and effectuate all necessary actions to guarantee adherence to the Social Responsibility Fund and approve funds for more expensive projects.

Despite all the controversy over the law, the actual content of media broadcasts has hardly changed, and perhaps the most noticeable difference since the law went into effect has been the announcement of explicit language

or graphic violence before certain programs. Like so many laws, its enforce-
ment will be as defining as its content, and it is too early to tell exactly how
the government intends to implement it. The vagueness of the language creates the space for the government to legally restrict speech in times where it
feels it is threatened, although the law is similar to laws in other democracies around the world, including France, the United Kingdom, and the
United States.

(69) How do international institutions and NGOs present this issue?

One of the most important international bodies to send delegations to evaluate freedom of speech in Venezuela and to meet with President Chávez on
the subject is the Inter-American Human Rights Commission (IHRC) of the
OAS. In a report published in 2003, the IHRC wrote:

> With respect to freedom of speech, the Commission, through
> its Freedom of Speech Council, has closely followed the pro-
> tection of this right in Venezuela. . . . The IHRC has confirmed
> that the government has not closed any newspapers nor
> arrested any journalists because of their political opinion.
> Nonetheless, freedom of speech is not limited to the absence of
> acts of censorship, the closing of newspapers, or arbitrary deten-
> tion of those who freely express their opinions. . . . [T]he lack
> of independence in the judiciary, the limitations on freedom of
> speech, the partisan role of the Armed Forces, the extreme
> polarization of society, the acts of death squads, the lack of
> credibility in state institutions due to uncertainty over the con-
> stitutionality of their appointments and the partisan nature of
> their actions, and the lack of coordination among security
> forces represent a clear weakness in the fundamental pillars of
> the rule of law in a democratic system as specified in the terms
> of the American Convention and the Inter-American Democ-
> ratic Charter.

The *Sociedad Interamericana de Prensa* (Inter-American Press Society,

IPS), an organization of the owners of the leading media outlets in the hemisphere, has been more decisive in their criticism of Venezuela's government. In March 2002 the IPS "expressed its grave concerns over the current situation with regard to freedom of speech in Venezuela and the ways in which it is being undermined along with the rule of law and the system of representative democracy." In September 2002, the group's spokespeople published a press release titled "IPS mission expresses its concerns and warns about the grave deterioration of the climate of freedom of the press in Venezuela." In March 2005 the group issued a statement including the following: "Venezuela is living under a dictatorial regime with Marxist aspirations. . . . In Venezuela there is an inhuman control of radio, TV, and Internet. . . . [President Chávez exercises] undue control over the judicial branch and overrides democratic guarantees for the media with the goal of consolidating his control over the government and the Armed Forces."

José Miguel Vivanco, executive director for the Americas division of Human Rights Watch, a global NGO, has regularly published his findings on human rights, especially freedom of speech, in Venezuela. In a press release in Washington on November 24, 2004, Vivanco denounced the recently approved media law: "This legislation severely threatens press freedom in Venezuela. . . . Its vaguely worded restrictions and heavy penalties are a recipe for self-censorship by the press and arbitrariness by government authorities. . . . Imposing a straitjacket on the media is not the way to promote democracy." In March 2005, he criticized the National Assembly's appointment of new justices to the Supreme Court for undermining the necessary impartiality of the court. He also criticized the penal code being debated in the National Assembly at the time (which President Chávez would later veto): "By broadening laws that punish disrespect for government authorities, the Venezuelan government has flouted international human rights principles that protect free expression. . . . These new provisions add to the arsenal of press restrictions already at the government's disposal. . . . By further criminalizing criticism of government authorities, these laws will restrict the public's ability to monitor abuse by those in power."

(70) Is there freedom of speech in Venezuela?

Venezuela has a vibrant public discourse, and all Venezuelans enjoy freedom of speech. The private media continues to vigorously attack the government, even as it claims freedom of speech no longer exists. There is not a single journalist in prison for his or her work or political opinion, and not a single private media outlet has been shut down or faced state intervention in its editorial policy. The government has not censored a single line or image from any of the country's print media.

Despite these facts, members of the private media in Venezuela, supported by the IPS, spokespeople from the White House, and various other international agencies, continue to denounce what they claim are threats to freedom of speech. Part of the problem, as mentioned above, is that in Venezuela, the media has long been linked to the ruling political parties, and media groups had become accustomed to wide powers and privileges—including substantial power over the appointment of government ministers, tax exemptions, and so forth. When President Chávez refused to extend these privileges, the media claimed it was under attack.

The media's ongoing campaign against the government, which in 2002 was able to play a major role in creating the political space for a short-lived coup and a prolonged national strike (see question 73), serves as a clear indication not only of the continued influence of the media, but also of its wide freedoms. For example, during the sixty-two days of the strike, all of the privately owned media suspended their regular programming to dedicate coverage to the effort to force President Chávez to resign. During these two months, the four leading TV channels in the capital transmitted 17,600 public announcements against the government (or 71 per channel per day, roughly one announcement every twenty minutes during the entire sixty-two days of the strike), and that does not include regional TV stations, print, or radio media.[14] Nonetheless, after the coup and the strike, none of the media outlets lost their broadcasting privileges or faced government intervention.

Oil

(71) **What are the prospects for the global energy industry?**

Oil will continue to be the energy source in greatest demand for years to come. Although projections suggest that natural gas consumption is on the rise, as is investment in renewable energy sources, the continued growth in the demand for petroleum-based energy resources is unparalleled. Both petroleum and natural gas are nonrenewable resources, and global reserves are rapidly being depleted.

The limited supply of energy reserves notwithstanding, the current spike in gas prices and the shortage of petroleum products are primarily a result of the lack of refining capacity. In other words, in the short term, the world's oil-refining capacity cannot keep up with either supply or demand. On April 25, 2005, Prince Bandar of Saudi Arabia emphasized the lack of refining capacity in a meeting in Crawford, Texas, when President Bush asked him to increase Saudi oil production. Over the long term, it is unlikely that supply of these nonrenewable resources will be able to keep up with rapidly increasing global demand, no matter what happens to refining capacity. Thus, energy has long been considered high politics, and global powers have been jockeying for geopolitical control of energy resources for well over 100 years.

The United States consumes more petroleum and natural gas than any other country in the world. With just 4 percent of the world's people, the United States consumes 26 percent of the petroleum, 45 percent of the gasoline, and 26 percent of the natural gas produced globally.[15] In 2001, according to President Bush's energy policy report, the United States had to import 60 of every 100 barrels of oil; that number was expected to grow to 75 barrels per 100 by the year 2020.

It is common knowledge the world over that President Bush's cabinet is largely composed of former oil executives. Further highlighting the significance of oil in geopolitics, most of the areas in the world engaged in armed conflict have significant energy reserves or serve as corridors for energy transport (including Sudan, Iraq, Afghanistan, and Colombia). According to a 2002 BP-Amoco report on global energy reserves, roughly 75 percent of proven petroleum reserves are located in the Middle East, while some 40 percent of natural gas is in Central Asia. In the Americas, the largest energy reserves are in the Andean-Amazonian arch, mostly divided between Venezuela (both petroleum and natural gas) and Bolivia (primarily natural gas reserves). Both of these countries have suffered from intense political instability in recent years, arguably caused in part by nationalist-oriented movements to gain control over these valuable natural resources. Ecuador and Colombia have smaller oil reserves that have also been linked to political instability.

Venezuela, located in the backyard of the United States, represents some of the largest energy reserves in the world. While a tanker takes roughly forty days to get to the U.S. coast from Saudi Arabia, it takes just five days from Venezuela. According to the minister of Energy and Mines, Venezuela has 78 billion barrels of proven petroleum reserves, and another 1.2 trillion barrels of unproven petroleum reserves, of which some 275 billion barrels are accessible with current drilling technology. (By way of comparison, Saudi Arabia has 270 billion barrels of proven reserves.) In addition, Venezuela has the eighth-largest natural gas reserves in the world, which it has only recently begun to exploit. Petroleum accounts for approximately one-third of GDP, 80 percent of export earnings, and 50 percent of government operating revenues, according to the CIA World Factbook on Venezuela. These statistics underscore the geostrategic importance of control over Venezuela's natural resources.

(72) How did PDVSA, a state-owned company, avoid working for the previous Venezuelan governments?

Under previous governments, executives in PDVSA had free rein to run the company as a state-within-a-state. Since President Chávez consolidated state control over the company, there have been numerous investigations into its operations over the previous thirty years. These investigations revealed information previously unknown to the general public and even to the rest of the government. According to some researchers, such as Carlos Mendoza Potellá, a professor at the Central University of Venezuela who has held a range of high-ranking positions within the Venezuelan oil industry, PDVSA's problems date all the way back to the nationalization of the oil industry in 1976.

At that time, the Venezuelan government selected the oil industry's leadership primarily from the ranks of the Venezuelan executives who had been running Exxon, Shell, and Gulf oil operations in Venezuela. Not surprisingly, the new PDVSA leadership and the transnational corporations they had worked for tended toward a common vision for Venezuela's oil industry. In other words, nationalization marked a dramatic shift in ownership, but a minor one in management. Once PDVSA was founded, its management quickly began competing for power with its parent Ministry of Energy and Mines. PDVSA's level of independence from the government can be roughly gauged by the share of its revenues that it pays to it. Ironically, nationalization set the company on a collision course with state interests: in 1981, PDVSA paid 71 cents on every dollar of gross revenue to the government, whereas in 2000, it paid just 39 cents on the dollar.

As failure after failure, scandal after scandal unfolded in governments during the Punto Fijo period, PDVSA executives developed policies to avoid paying money into the corrupt and inefficient governments. In 1983 the company began a massive internationalization campaign; to prevent the government from demanding PDVSA's liquid assets, the company decided not to have any. As Bernard Mommer, vice minister of energy and mines, puts it, "Internationalization was devised by PDVSA to create a conveyor belt to relocate profits out of the reach of the government through transfer pricing (i.e., the price charged by one affiliate to another affiliate in the accounts of the parent company)."[16] By 1989, they had successfully invested the majority of the country's oil wealth—billions of dollars—overseas in some 184 companies and paved the way for reprivatization through a series of joint ventures with private transnational firms.

One example of this policy was the acquisition of and investment in the Citgo refinery and distribution network in the United States. Not only did PDVSA spend millions on expanding its filling stations and refineries, but it also signed long-term supply contracts with its new subsidiary guaranteeing crude supplies at well below market values for years to come. By the late 1990s, PDVSA was using this internal contract system to remit roughly $500 million a year to its foreign affiliates, out of the reach of the Venezuelan government. By the time President Chávez took office, the company had managed to acquire nearly $10 billion in debt. As Mommer explains:

> For eighteen years after the beginning of internationalization, the foreign affiliates of PDVSA never paid dividends to the holding company in Caracas. But earning profits for the country was never the objective of the policy in the first place. In December 2001 the Chávez government obliged the foreign affiliates to pay dividends for the first time.

When the Chávez government decided it was time for PDVSA to start working for Venezuela instead of the other way around, it met fierce resistance from the company's leadership. In early 2002, this tension led President Chávez to replace many of the company's top executives, who would retaliate in the April 2002 coup, quickly followed by the December 2002 oil strike. Although PDVSA continues to be the focus of debate, the company now works for the benefit of Venezuela.

(73) What was the December 2002 oil strike?

After the failed April 2002 coup, the government continued to deepen the revolution, and the opposition continued their fight to bring down the government. In early December 2002, the opposition initiated what would prove to be another attempt to force President Chávez to resign. This attempt involved many of the same conspirators: Fedecámaras, CTV, and former executives from PDVSA joined together in a triad they called the

Democratic Coordinator. They organized a national strike in key industries such as energy, petrochemicals, transportation, and food distribution; ultimately, companies and businesses in almost every sector of the economy joined in or were forced to close for lack of electricity and fuel. For those supporting the campaign, it represented a well-coordinated, peaceful, democratic expression of dissent in the form of a national work stoppage determined to force the government from office, no matter the cost. For those supporting the government, it represented the longest, most sustained sabotage campaign in the country's history and has come to be known as the "oil coup" or the "oil sabotage."

The plan was put into action when the opposition executives and managers who were still within the ranks of PDVSA told the people working under them at PDVSA installations and administrative offices across the country not to come to work. Those who tried to go to work were locked out and threatened with termination of their contracts, even when failure to operate plants or wells resulted in irreversible losses to the national industry. Intesa, the company responsible for PDVSA's information systems, was among the many companies that joined the strike, leaving the government with no way to even begin to control this important state-owned industry. Intesa's control of the company was so extensive that then president of PDVSA Alí Rodríguez Araque (now the foreign minister) was left without access to his own personal computer.

The striking managers were able to freeze activity in wells, petrochemical treatment plants, refineries, and loading docks throughout the country. On December 9, 2002, in the midst of the strike, Minister of Energy and Mines Rafael Ramírez argued that in many cases the strike had morphed into criminal sabotage: "They destroyed refining ovens through rapid changes in internal temperature, they left tanks of asphalt solidifying, they left chemicals coagulating in pipes."

Venezuela went from being the world's fifth-leading oil exporter to buying oil on the international market in order to meet its contractual obligations with foreign clients. Oil production decreased from around 3 million barrels per day to a low of 25,000 barrels per day. In the aftermath of the strike, the damage was calculated at more than $15 billion, much of which was permanent damage to machinery and petroleum-processing technology.

The shortage of refined petroleum products had ripple effects throughout the entire country, undermining the operational capacity of the armed forces and creating a nationwide food shortage. The strike led to extreme shortages of gasoline and diesel fuels, so that lines at filling stations throughout the country were miles long. Thousands of families began cooking with firewood because of the power outages and lack of cooking gas. Venezuela's international credit rating plummeted, and thousands of small businesses failed.

The strike lasted for sixty-two days. During that time, the government, with the support of the armed forces and workers in every industry, struggled to regain control of the country. Workers in industries like trucking, refining, and information technology broke into their own workplaces to get the wheels of the economy spinning, even in the face of intimidation from the strike's organizers, and have become national heroes as a result.

The government fired some nineteen thousand members of PDVSA's management and staff who'd supported the oil strike. Roughly half of these were later replaced, and the others were written off as unnecessary bureaucracy. Despite the reduction in management staff, the government claims to have brought oil production back up to full capacity and has converted one of the old management-office complexes in Caracas for use by the new UBV.

(74) What is "Petroamérica"?

President Chávez's idea, known as Petroamérica, is to develop a strategic alliance with other countries in the Americas to strengthen each other through regional integration of energy production and distribution. Although this ambitious project is still a long way from coming to fruition, Venezuela has taken crucial first steps toward it in the form of a series of bilateral energy treaties.

According to Chávez's vision, energy cooperation can be used as an engine to drive social development throughout the region. He hopes to make petroleum a natural resource that directly benefits the people who own it. In Latin America, as in much of the developing world, natural resources have long served only to benefit the foreign companies that extract them and a small domestic elite, and to improve the country's macroeconomic indicators, without actually benefiting the majority of people, who live in poverty. In this case the idea is to use the exportation of a valuable raw material to develop other areas of the national and regional economy so that these relatively weak nations can gain control of their own development.

Through contracts for exploration, production, and sales, PDVSA has already begun integrating with Enarsa, Argentina's state-owned oil company, and Petrobras, Brazil's state-owned oil company. In February 2005, PDVSA opened an office and its first gas stations in Argentina, which it hopes to expand to a national network of some six hundred filling stations throughout Argentina as a major step toward the creation of Petroamérica.

Many countries in the region have suffered tremendously under the strain of neoliberal structural adjustments imposed by the IMF, the World Bank, and other international financial institutions as conditions for loans. The Argentine economic crisis in 2001 is often cited as an example of this trend. It is in this regional context that President Chávez proposes to use the region's most valuable natural resource to break a historic dependency on foreign capital and to simultaneously solve an ongoing social crisis, all in the spirit of Simón Bolívar's vision of regional unity.

Although this vision has been much more thoroughly developed in President Chávez's speeches than in the real world, Venezuela has signed a series of bilateral energy treaties with Brazil, Argentina, Uruguay, Paraguay, Cuba, and Trinidad that could serve as the building blocks for deeper integration. In July 2005, Chávez won a political victory in negotiations toward "Petrocaribe," which will form part of broader Petroamérica, and the Bolivarian Alternative for the Americas (ALBA). The agreement provides Caribbean countries with below market prices on oil imports from Venezuela, solidifies Venezuela's dominance in easy to reach, small markets, and gives Chávez political leverage in the region. President Chávez has even talked about the need to expand this energy cooperation to include countries throughout the global south, and his visits to China and India in 2005 were intended to set the stage for south-south integration—as is his pending tour of Africa.

(75) Is it true that Venezuela gives free oil to Cuba?

Venezuela provides Cuba with preferential conditions for its oil imports, but their agreement does not constitute free oil. In fact, Venezuela has signed three major energy treaties with its Central American and Caribbean neighbors: the San José Accord (1980), the Caracas Energy Cooperation Accord (2000), and the Cuban-Venezuelan Petroleum Pact (2000), which is simply an extension of the Caracas Energy Cooperation Accord.

The San José Accord, developed with Mexico, commits these oil exporters to cooperate in providing Caribbean and Central American countries with below-market prices on small-scale oil imports for domestic consumption. Eleven countries benefit from this accord, among them El Salvador, Guatemala, Costa Rica, Panama, Nicaragua, the Dominican Republic, and Haiti.

The Caracas Energy Cooperation Accord, for which Venezuela is the only oil producer, provides up to 160,000 barrels per day of Venezuelan crude oil with fifteen-year financing, an interest rate of 2 percent a year, and price caps. The countries party to this accord include Nicaragua, Belize, Costa Rica, El Salvador, Guatemala, Panama, the Dominican Republic, Guyana, Grenada, and St. Vincent and the Grenadines.

The Cuban-Venezuelan Petroleum Pact is based closely on the Caracas Energy Cooperation Accord, but forms part of a comprehensive series of bilateral treaties between these two Caribbean neighbors. Some critics have suggested that Cuba resells Venezuelan oil on the international market for a profit. The numbers disprove this assertion: Cuban domestic consumption of petroleum is roughly 170,000 barrels per day, of which 70,000 barrels are produced domestically. Hence, Cuba must import approximately 100,000 barrels of oil per day to meet its energy requirements. Cuba's treaty with Venezuela provides for preferential terms on up to 53,000 barrels per day, which means Cuba still must buy some 47,000 barrels of oil per day on the spot market or meet this requirement through other treaties.

What separates the treaty with Cuba from Venezuela's two other regional energy agreements is the fact that it goes beyond energy relations. In exchange for the preferential buying conditions, and mitigated by a series of other conditions and treaties, Cuba provides Venezuela with significant personnel and resource support for its public health system, its educational system, and its sports programs.

Venezuela does not give away its oil; nor does it exchange it for Cuban medicine. Cuba pays for the oil it imports from Venezuela, just as Venezuela pays for the goods and services it receives from Cuba. These treaties represent mutually beneficial trade accords not unlike those every country in the world seeks with its neighbors and allies.

(76) **What kinds of investments does the Venezuelan government have in the United States?**

The United States is one of the countries that receives the most beneficial prices on Venezuelan oil. Through a series of long-term supply contracts with guaranteed below-market prices, Venezuela provides greater subsidies on its exports to the United States than it does to Cuba or to any of the countries that benefit from the San José Accord or the Caracas Energy Cooperation Accord.

Venezuela has invested more than $12 billion in the United States through its refineries, terminals, and related facilities. These investments have created more than 150,000 jobs in the United States, according to Congressman Bill Delahunt. Venezuela's primary investment in the United States is the Citgo Petroleum Corporation, headquartered in Houston, Texas. The fourth-largest fuel retailer in the United States, Citgo is owned by PDV America, Inc., a wholly owned subsidiary of PDVSA. In other words, PDVSA is the sole owner of Citgo, its fourteen thousand filling sta-tions, and eight refineries. Including joint-venture projects, Citgo has a refining capacity of some 1.1 million barrels of crude oil per day.

In early 2005, rumors about a possible sale of Citgo began to circulate. President Chávez expressed interest in selling part of Citgo to another oil company and redefining its supply contracts with PDVSA. He complained that Citgo pays below-market prices for its crude oil purchases, which shifts profits away from PDVSA and its owner, the Venezuelan government. By concentrating profits directly within PDVSA instead of in its subsidiary, the Venezuelan government hopes to avoid paying millions of dollars in taxes to the U.S. government.

As Rafael Ramírez, minister of Energy and Mines and president of PDVSA, put it in an interview with *El Universal* on April 18, 2005, "We cannot go on subsidizing the most powerful economy in the world; it makes no sense." Ramírez went on to say that Venezuela intends to sell two of its U.S.-based Citgo refineries as part of an internal reform process to make Citgo more prof-itable for Venezuela, and to focus Citgo's refining capacity exclusively on Venezuelan crude oil. Analysts expect PDVSA to sell the 167,000-barrels-a-day Lemont, Illinois, refinery, which processed no Venezuelan crude in 2004, instead relying on crude oil purchased from other countries. The minister argued that the two refineries in question "are of no interest to us because they systematically produce financial losses, because they do not refine our petroleum." Given the drastic shortage of refining capacity in the United States driving gas prices to record highs, Venezuela has had no trouble attracting potential buyers. Still, as of July 2005, no significant progress had been made in the potential sale, and Ramírez has repeatedly denied that Venezuela intends to sell its other U.S.-based investments.

(77) How has Venezuela's oil policy changed under Chávez?

Under previous governments, PDVSA had been run as an independent, private company, despite the fact that it has always been fully owned by the Venezuelan government. Nonetheless, PDVSA executives regularly had larger salaries and more bodyguards than the government ministers responsible for overseeing PDVSA.

In general, PDVSA was a closed-door, entirely opaque state-owned company. Most Venezuelans had no idea how the company operated or how its operations impacted them, and PDVSA executives intended to keep it that way. Skilled workers within PDVSA were generally paid quite well, but rather than benefiting all Venezuelans who own the oil that PDVSA produces, a narrow labor elite was created.

The old PDVSA was essentially a transnational company that managed to avoid paying dividends or even disclosing all of its accounting records to its sole shareholder. It was given total independence to negotiate contracts, determine executive compensation, manage labor relations, invest its earnings, and pay dividends as it saw fit.

Now, although PDVSA employees continue to receive some of the highest salaries in the country, even when compared to people who do exactly the same job for a different state-owned company, the company's leadership has a different vision of its role in Venezuelan society. PDVSA has become the leading funder of the government's massive national social programs. Instead of focusing its resources on foreign investments and acquisitions, PDVSA now directs its profits toward the development and diversification of the Venezuelan economy—both through investment in other sectors of national industry and through a series of new international alliances with countries like China and India. With PDVSA's support,

Venezuela is preparing to launch its first satellite, built in China, and to develop its own line of automobiles with Iranian technology.

(78) How did Venezuela contribute to the launching and the relaunching of OPEC?

Venezuela was one of the countries that organized the founding of OPEC at the Baghdad Conference in 1960. Nonetheless, PDVSA's free market–oriented leadership under previous governments developed export policies that went directly against the interests of the oil cartel. Instead of limiting exports to keep global market prices high, the old PDVSA's policy was to maximize volume to increase gross sales. Thus, Venezuela quickly went from being a founding member of OPEC to being a rogue member that regularly violated its quotas.

By the early 1990s, the price of oil on the world market had dropped to historic lows. When President Chávez took office, the price had bottomed out at $7 per barrel, or just above the cost of production for most wells. These prices led to a dramatic increase in oil consumption in countries like the United States, but nearly bankrupted the Venezuelan government, which is highly dependent on oil profits. Ironically, Venezuela's state-owned oil company had actively contributed to driving down prices on the world market.

Venezuela's relationship with OPEC made a dramatic shift in the wake of President Chávez's election. In his campaign, he argued for a return to price-protection policies. During his first year in office, President Chávez visited ten members of OPEC in order to personally assure his counterparts of Venezuela's commitment to their common cause and his vision for OPEC in the twenty-first century. In the fall of 2000, Venezuela hosted an OPEC summit and was elected to the presidency of the organization, which represented a vote of confidence in Venezuela's ability to lead the organization's efforts to bring oil prices back up.

The United States and the European Union have long been critical of OPEC's efforts to drive up oil prices. The U.S. government has pressured OPEC to increase its production quotas in order to lower prices. Venezuela promotes the current quotas, pointing out that a large percentage of the retail cost of fuel in the United States and the European Union is actually government-imposed taxes, not product cost.

The cooperation of OPEC members in not overselling their quotas was crucial in driving the price of a barrel of oil back up to the cartel's established price band of between $22 and $28 per barrel. Prices continued to rise quickly in the wake of the attacks on September 11, 2001, and the subsequent U.S. invasions of Afghanistan and Iraq. In August 2005, oil markets reached historic highs, with the price of a barrel above $70. Though a complex range of factors contributed to the rise in oil prices, the relaunching of OPEC as a major player in international oil markets certainly played a role. Unity within OPEC would not have been possible without Venezuela's leadership.

(79) How does the opposition view the new PDVSA?

PDVSA is slowly being integrated into a new vision of the Venezuelan state. For the capitalist-oriented members of the opposition, who had greatly benefited from a PDVSA independent of its owner—from the status quo—few things about the Chávez government are more frightening. This is, however, rarely the language used to criticize the new PDVSA. On any given day, the private media reports dozens of opposition criticisms of government oil policy. Rather than compiling an exhaustive list of all of the opposition statements with regard to PDVSA, this answer uses one day, May 27, 2005, as an example.

On May 27, Oswaldo Álvarez Paz, the 1988 presidential candidate for the COPEI party, was quoted in several newspapers calling on all Venezuelans to close ranks with regard to the oil industry because "if we unify our criteria and our forces, between all of us we can ensure that either the government changes its attitude or we will change the government." He went on to say that PDVSA's "freedom has been limited by ongoing [government] interventions," its atmosphere politicized, and its resources used to finance the president's personal budget so that the company "is now at the point of bankruptcy, under assault, and in ruins." Humberto Calderón Berti, a former president of PDVSA and OPEC, said, "The country has no idea how bad PDVSA is right now. No one knows what is happening because PDVSA's resources are being spent without any controls."

Likewise, Antonio Ledezma, former leader of the AD party who recently founded the Alliance of the Brave People Party, went to the Supreme Court to request that it annul a resolution passed by the central bank allowing

PDVSA to create an account maintained in dollars. Ledezma argued that PDVSA's management was incompetent and that "the money was being used without any kind of control or supervision." José Agustín Gómez, a leader of the party Just One People, went so far as to request the resignation of the president of PDVSA and the entire board of directors, whom he accused of being corrupt and inept. He requested that the attorney general open an investigation into the accounting throughout the national oil industry to uncover proof of the alleged corruption.

Finally, the daily newspaper *El Nacional* ran a front-page headline declaring, "Fires forced the oil port in Zulia to close," indicating managerial incompetence as the cause of a fire and citing a Reuters newswire for the story. Reuters denied having reported the port closure, though it affirmed, "That story certainly came across our wires, but it was from May 27th of last year [2004]." PDVSA also released information showing that the port in Zulia was operating at normal capacity. Eventually *El Nacional* issued a retraction. This kind of apocalyptic misreporting has become commonplace; the retractions, however, are less common.

(80) **What is the mandate of the new PDVSA?**

After the failure of the December 2002 oil strike, the government won new-found control over PDVSA and began using its control of this lucrative industry to invest oil rents in projects designed to fulfill the social guarantees of the Bolivarian Constitution. This mandate represents a dramatic change from the old PDVSA, which systematically undermined consecutive governments through flawed oil policy and eventually actively participated in a series of attempts to overthrow the democratically elected president.

The new PDVSA is a public company that invests its earnings in developing Venezuela with the goal of breaking its historic dependence on a mono-export. This ambitious project to diversify and industrialize the economy was simply not possible until the government gained control of PDVSA and helped drive up world oil prices. Venezuela's government is "sowing" the country's oil with an eye toward the future not only of a narrow economic elite or the oil industry, but of the entire country. Oil money is now funding the missions, generating employment in sectors well beyond the oil industry, financing job training and the development of cooperatives and small businesses, supporting the expansion of Venezuela's agricultural industry, purchasing modern light arms for the military, and facilitating a series of international treaties designed to guarantee Venezuela's independence and sovereignty.

Under previous leaderships, PDVSA's resources were invested in the company's foreign holdings, rather than in the Venezuelan people and economy. Now the policy objective for PDVSA is to finance the development of a diversified economy and a massive social service campaign. According to PDVSA's propaganda: the new PDVSA is at the service of all of Venezuela.

ECONOMY AND LAND REFORM

(81) **What is Venezuela's current economic model?**

Historically, Venezuela's economic model was based closely on leading economic theory from Western economic institutions. Thus, in the 1980s and 1990s the government followed the structural adjustment guidelines of international financial institutions based on improving macroeconomic indicators, reducing public services, increasing direct foreign investment, and privatizing the economy.

Under this economic model, by 1997, the wealthiest 5 percent of the country had incomes that were 53.1 times greater than the poorest 5 percent; roughly 85 percent of the country lived in poverty and 67 percent lived in extreme poverty, earning less than $2 per day. Over half of the workforce was in the informal economy. According to the World Bank, by 2003 the richest 20 percent received 53 percent of national income while the poorest 20 percent received just 3 percent. Despite the serious social costs and widespread popular resistance—like the *Caracazo*—this policy trend continued right up until President Chávez's election and, as the above statistics indicate, the social tendencies it established continued well into his first term.

During his campaign, President Chávez argued for an alternative to the neoliberal model and its shock therapy—which is largely absorbed by the poor and lower middle class. The drafters of the Bolivarian Constitution tried to create a humanist model based on meeting the people's needs. The constitution's humanist guarantees aside, six years into the Chávez administration, it is still unclear exactly what economic model is being implemented. In early 2005 President Chávez began to talk more and more about developing a twenty-first-century model of socialism. When he talks about this socialist model, he refrains from clearly defining it and instead tends to call for debate and research into how to best develop an alternative to capitalism that also avoids the errors of previous socialist experiments.

Despite Chávez's call for a move toward socialism, the Venezuelan economy is still capitalist both in theory—in articles 112 and 115 the constitution clearly defends individual economic rights and private property—and in practice—the vast majority of the means of production are privately owned. On the other hand, the same constitution that enshrines private property makes references to the value of cooperatives in article 118, and the government has long owned (since well before Chávez was elected) the most lucrative industry in the country: oil. Transnational oil companies control a large share of the oil industry, but must be licensed to work under PDVSA. All of this creates a bit of a conundrum when it comes to defining the Venezuelan economy in absolute terms. Venezuelan economist Luis Damiani argues that Venezuela is in the midst of a transition to socialism in which transnational investors, local capitalists, cooperative enterprises, and comanaged factories exist side by side.

(82) What is the government's international finance policy?

As this book went to press, Venezuela's public debt was roughly $33 billion, of which $22 billion was external debt. The $33 billion figure is often cited as external debt, but the government has made an effort to convert its external debt to internal debt through a series of buybacks and new dollarized bond sales made available to local investors. Rather than depend on foreign investors to finance state operations and debt restructuring, Venezuela has increasingly turned to domestic financiers.

The Chávez government has avoided acquiring any significant new debt from international financial institutions, but it has continued to service its debt. In other words, despite Chávez's "drop the debt" campaign rhetoric, and his ongoing criticisms of the IMF and the World Bank, his government regularly pays down its external debt in accordance with the terms of the loans taken on under previous governments. As Chávez explains it:

> Now, maybe if you told me that the global context, or at least the regional context, began to change, and that a large group of countries began to move toward a position that allowed us more strength and flexibility, things would be different. If a political leadership rose up willing to face the risk together and explain their common decision to the world, to organize an OHIC, if you will allow me to invent a name here—Organization of Highly Indebted Countries, that ought to include Mexico, Argentina, Brazil, Venezuela, etc., then we could sit down together, five or six presidents, and tell the world that we are calling a meeting with the owners of banks A, B, C, D, because between us we owe them something like $100 billion and we would tell them: "OK, gentlemen, we have made a decision in the name of our 200 or 300 million citizens who elected us to govern them, to represent their interests. We want to pay the debt, but not as it is. We demand a change in the system of payment." Under conditions like those I have just laid out, with a more favorable balance of power, we might be able to accomplish something.
>
> We could decisively, clearly say that we will not pay the debt, but I prefer a conciliatory path. So what are the available conciliatory paths? Well, there are plenty, actually. One is called the International Humanitarian Fund: we sign an agreement saying that we legitimately owe X percent of the debt but we have already paid it three times over and we are still in debt, it is eternal as Fidel has said, so we put the money in a fund that a UN-appointed board can administer to fight poverty in our own countries and in neighboring countries.[17]

Chávez is highly aware of the importance of maintaining good standing in international financial markets, which Venezuela has been able to do, thanks largely to regularly meeting its scheduled payments, and to its record-high federal reserves, totaling more than the country's external debt. As a Moody's financial group analysis released on May 16, 2005, put it, "Venezuela's foreign-currency debt rating of B2 and stable outlook are supported by a demonstrated policy of servicing public-sector debt in full and on a timely basis and a strong foreign-exchange reserve position. Venezuela's policy on foreign exchange and capital controls has provided foreign-exchange authorizations for servicing private-sector debt on a timely basis." Moody's vice president Luis Ernesto Martinez-Alas added that "Moody's ratings and outlook reflect our view that foreign-exchange controls reduce the possibility of a sharp and sudden decline in international reserves, even in the event of falling oil prices." Venezuela's total foreign-exchange reserves are estimated to exceed $30 billion.

(83) What is endogenous development?

Endogenous means originating from within, and endogenous development means development from within. The national government has chosen this model for its plan to diversify and develop Venezuela's economy beyond the mono-export of petroleum. This model is not one that Washington or international financial institutions, quick to involve themselves in domestic-development policy of weak countries, have ever promoted. Rather it is, like so much else in Venezuela, a model that the Bolivarian Revolution is inventing as it goes along.

Endogenous development does, however, resemble a development model known as import substitution, popular in Latin America beginning in the 1950s and continuing into the early 1980s. In import substitution, underdeveloped economies import the technology to develop industry and modernize their country. Chávez has distinguished endogenous development from import substitution, pointing out that "one of the causes of the failure of the import substitution model was that it sought to copy the production model from developed countries, without taking into consideration our own" unique circumstances.

According to a government economic-policy advisor, "Endogenous development has to do with sovereignty—with the ability to develop based on our own needs, using our own resources and our own projects. But, it's not about isolation. It's not about rejecting the idea of exporting. Certainly, it's not about refusing to sell oil and other natural resources when we can use those sales to develop and to reduce in this way our dependence upon oil."[18]

The Venezuelan government presents endogenous development as an alternative to the neoliberal economic model, which took such a heavy toll on Venezuela's poor in the 1980s and 1990s. In June 2004, as he often does, President Chávez defined endogenous development by explaining what it is not: "Endogenous development is the antithesis of exogenous development, in which all of the impulses come from outside, a model that depends on foreign capital, on foreign banks, on foreign markets, on foreign technology. [Exogenous development] is a model that puts the people of each country against each other to see who can produce the most cheaply for foreign markets, who can drive wages, social and environmental conditions the lowest to win the war of everyone against everyone. Neoliberalism promotes the race to the bottom and exogenous development is its model."[19] In Venezuela, endogenous development is a socio-economic model that encourages communities to put forward their own development proposals.

The government is trying to expedite the implementation of its endogenous development model through Mission Vuelvan Caras (see question 46). Participants in the mission organize themselves into cooperatives based on areas of economic activity and their networks of cooperatives form endogenous development nuclei. The government provides loans and technical support for these endogenous development nuclei and cooperatives, consistent with article 116 of the constitution, as a way to reduce unemployment and strengthen Venezuela's economy and national sovereignty.

(84) What is the process for urban land reform?

During the petroleum boom that began in the 1960s, Venezuelans began migrating en masse to urban areas, particularly Caracas, in the hopes of a better quality of life. Because of the spontaneous nature of this internal migration, the rapid expansion of the cities without planned development—or in many cases even basic services—led to the proliferation of densely populated sectors known as barrios.

The trend toward urbanization continued even after the oil boom ended.

The percentage of the labor force that worked in the agricultural sector decreased from 16.1 percent in 1980 to 10 percent in 1997, and from 1989 to 1992 some 600,000 people abandoned the countryside. By 2003, 88 percent of the country lived in urban areas.[20] Many of these people arrived in the cities broke and without anywhere to live, so they often set up shantytowns on whatever open space they could find. While these shantytowns started off as nothing but cardboard and tin shacks, they slowly expanded into overpopulated brick structures that surround most of Venezuela's cities, and now creep dangerously high up into the hills overlooking Caracas.

The Chávez government, recognizing the precarious living situation of the majority of its population, decided to regularize urban land holdings. This process, similar to what Peruvian development economist Hernando de Soto argues for (see *The Mystery of Capital: Why Capitalism Works in the West and Fails Everywhere Else*, for example), gives the poor people living on small plots of land for years official legal title to what is already unofficially theirs. Unlike de Soto's model, which is largely state driven, the Venezuelan approach is bottom-up. According to decree 1,666, published on February 4, 2002, urban dwellers seeking legal title to their land are required to organize into Urban Land Committees representing up to two hundred families with a board of directors of between seven and eleven members elected by a simple majority of the families forming the committee.

Once the committees are organized, they are registered with the National Technical Office for Urban Land Regularization, which then helps them survey their land and mark off borders. Once the survey process, difficult in the unplanned and disorganized barrios, is completed, the committees are given provisional titles that are only formalized and finalized after a three-month waiting period. During those three months, any disputes must be settled and anyone laying claim to the land outside of the committee must present their original title. As stipulated in article 1 of decree 1,666, the committees also have the obligation to submit their charters and titles for formal incorporation into the government's urban land regularization legal code so that norms and procedures for recognition of land acquisition rights, and use of public lands, can be legally defined as the process moves forward.

This urban land reform process is considerably more profound than the simple issue of legal title to land—it has served to organize the people in the barrios and encouraged them to engage in Venezuela's new participatory democracy. The same committees form the basis for self-managed communities as well as liaisons to state institutions and service providers. They are well positioned to identify their own problems and request the support of the state when and where it is needed. These same committees are charged with writing neighborhood charters and enforcing them.

Beyond the regularization of urban land and the political involvement it brings about, this process also has the potential to serve as an economic stimulus in poor urban communities. Hernando de Soto argues that legal title will enable even the poorest people to use their homes as guarantees to obtain microcredit. As writer and sociologist Gregory Wilpert, who has spent years in Venezuela, puts it, this microcredit may "generate a boom in the economy of the barrio."

(85) How is agrarian reform being implemented?

Venezuela's land has been concentrated in the hands of the few, and worked by the many, since it was first partitioned out under the Spanish *hacienda* system. The inefficient, unjust, exploitative distribution of land changed little over the centuries, even after independence. The first major government effort to redistribute the land did not come until 1960, as one of the first steps taken by the newly democratic government. The agrarian reform law put in place by presidential decree sought to redistribute the land and make it more productive. This law was the first major step toward a modernized countryside, including the creation of several agrarian-oriented state institutions.

As the years passed, successive governments did not follow up on the agrarian reform : process initiated in 1960. This lack of follow-up was possible, in part, because Venezuela was in the midst of a rapid urbanization process—power, politics, and people came to be focused in a few urban centers totally removed from the countryside. The abandonment of the countryside by both the people and the government made food production more and more difficult. Small landowners often opted to sell their parcels and move to the cities. This tendency reversed the redistributive efforts of the 1960 agrarian reform law.

The urbanization process accelerated in the 1970s. Oil rents made agriculture largely unnecessary in Venezuela as the urban population found it just as easy to import food from abroad as from their own countryside. Thus the agricultural sector passed from representing 50 percent of GDP in 1960 to representing 6.1 percent in 2004, the lowest in Latin America.[21]

The Bolivarian Constitution includes several articles that lay out a vision for rural development. Article 306 is emblematic: "The State shall promote conditions for overall rural development, for the purpose of generating employment and ensuring the rural population an adequate level of well-being, as well as their inclusion in national development. It shall likewise promote agricultural activity and optimum land use by providing infrastructure projects, supplies, loans, training services, and technical assistance."

To try to live up to this constitutional mandate, the government has put in place a series of policies to support the agricultural sector, including low-interest loans, rural-infrastructure development projects, forced sales and redistribution of fallow land, and international treaties aimed at supporting rural development. For example, in the spring of 2005 Venezuela and Iran inaugurated a joint-venture project: the VENIRAN tractor factory. Venezuela has also signed a series of agreements with China to assemble agricultural products in Venezuela. These agreements accomplish several goals at once: they strengthen Venezuela's industrial base, consolidate strong bilateral relations, expand strategic industries in the interest of national security, and, of course, support the rebirth of an agricultural sector.

One of the most controversial of the forty-nine enabling laws put in place in November 2001 was the Land Law, which replaced the 1960 agrarian reform law and arguably played a key role in setting the stage for the coup because of the resistance it engendered. In its efforts to tackle the second-highest concentration of land in Latin America—70 percent of arable land was controlled by just 3 percent of landowners—the Land Law set maximum limits on the size of farms. The limits ranged from one hundred hectares to five thousand hectares, depending on the quality of land and the level of productivity.

In early 2005, the Supreme Court found parts of this law to be incompatible with the constitution's private property guarantees, and thus some of these specifications have been changed. The Land Law also provided for a special inactivity tax for landowners who failed to use more than 80 percent of their land and encouraged redistribution to small farmers. Article 14 of the law took unprecedented steps in defending the role of women in the countryside by prioritizing female heads-of-household land claims and guaranteeing rural mothers pre- and postnatal loans.

(86) **Does the government respect private property?**

The international community has been anxious about Venezuela's willing-ness to defend private property rights. International media attention has been focused on Venezuela particularly since January 2005, when the British-owned El Charcote cattle ranch in central Venezuela started making headlines. Peasant squatters had already been occupying much of the ranch for several years, but in January 2005, the Venezuelan government finished an investigation that found that the Vestey's meat group, with roughly 1,350 square miles of land divided up among thirteen cattle farms including El Charcote, did not have clear legal title to parts of the land it claimed, and that it was failing to use the land efficiently. The government repossessed the untitled land, promptly titled it to peasant families, and forced a sale of the land it found to be fallow. Vestey's was given sixty days to appeal, in accor-dance with the law. The international news media began to grumble.

Though both the government and its critics present El Charcote ranch as an example of land-distribution policy, the fact is that respect for private property is clearly enshrined in the constitution. Article 115 reads as follows:

> The right of property is guaranteed. Every person has the right to the use, enjoyment, usufruct, and disposal of his or her goods. Property shall be subject to such contributions, restrictions, and obligations as may be established by law in the service of the public or general interest. Only for reasons of public benefit or social interest by final judgment, with timely payment of fair compensation, the expropriation of any kind of property may be declared.

Despite this clear guarantee, the article introduces a catena because prop-erty "shall be subject to such contributions, restrictions, and obligations as may be established by law." The laws on the books create stipulations that allow, as in the case of El Charcote, where it is to the "public benefit or social interest," for the government to expropriate land—by "final judgment, with timely payment of fair compensation." Landowners are paid the current market value for their property, usually based on value listed for tax purposes. Large landowners who undervalue their property to avoid paying taxes are bound to be unhappy with the price the government offers.

For many international observers, these qualifications go too far in under-mining private property; however, for many domestic supporters of the dem-ocratic revolution, the government is far too generous in compensating exploitative landowners. Aside from the issues over the forced sales of fallow land, Venezuela respects, defends, and indeed is based on a system of private property.

(87) What is Venezuela's food-security doctrine?

The idea of food security has been debated within the Venezuelan Left for years, and has been on the government's agenda since Chávez's first presi-dential campaign in 1998. For the Chávez administration food security, or the ability to meet Venezuela's food consumption needs from within, through comprehensive rural development, is a strategic priority. Tradition-ally Venezuela has imported approximately 80 percent of its food from abroad despite its rich soil and water sources.

The food-security doctrine is built into the Bolivarian Constitution and is clearly articulated in article 305:

> The State shall promote sustainable agriculture as the strategic basis for overall rural development, and consequently shall guar-antee the population a secure food supply, defined as the suffi-cient and stable availability of food within the national sphere and timely and uninterrupted access to the same for consumers. A secure food supply must be achieved by developing and prior-itizing internal agricultural and livestock production, under-stood as production deriving from the activities of agriculture, livestock, fishing, and aquaculture. Food production is in the national interest and is fundamental to the economic and social development of the Nation. To this end, the State shall promul-gate such financial, commercial, technological transfer, land tenancy, infrastructure, manpower training, and other measures as may be necessary to achieve strategic levels of self-sufficiency. In addition, it shall promote actions in the national and interna-tional economic context to compensate for the disadvantages inherent to agricultural activity.

The State shall protect the settlement and communities of nonindustrialized fishermen, as well as their fishing banks in continental waters and those close to the coastline, as defined by law.

This article details the government's strategic food objectives, many of which have been put in action through the agrarian reform process discussed above. On the distribution and consumption side of the food industry, Mission Mercal (see question 47) has been the primary government vehicle to stabilize prices and secure consumer markets. There is clear strategic value to having a broad, stable food-production base within the country, as the food shortages during the December 2002 national strike proved. Still, the fact that Venezuelans prefer flour to corn, Coca-Cola and a hamburger to *mora* juice and an *arepa* means that it will take much more than just good agricultural policy to support a domestic food-production base. Despite the government's concrete steps, it is still a long way from meeting its objectives, and Venezuelan consumer trends will have to change dramatically if it is to even stand a chance.

(88) What are the primary successes and failures of the new political economy?

Any discussion of successes and failures in a field as complex and politicized as economics depends dramatically on one's perspective and on one's values. The government often presents certain developments as successes even as the opposition criticizes the same facts or events as major failures. Statistics can be helpful in getting past the politics, but they can also be deceiving, and their value is greatly diminished when describing a process that purports to be innovating an alternative economic model over the long term.

The government has presented the implementation of its economic model—one that puts the economy at the service of the majority instead of the minority—as a success. According to the government, the successes include a focus on the growth of cooperatives, on the increase in sustainable small-scale agricultural and fishing collectives, and on the long-term investment in education and health care for the poorest sectors of society. The government is attempting to plan for the day when oil reserves run out by investing heavily in the citizenry and in alternate sectors of the economy. In terms of its macroeconomic indicators, the government places its economic progress, its level of direct foreign investment, its growth rates, inflation, and so on, in the context of a series of sustained attacks and internal sabotage designed to destroy not only the government in power but also the country's most valuable industries.

Even with the virtually continuous problems the government has faced, in 2004 the economy grew by 17.3 percent, the highest growth rate in the region, and the highest in the sixty-four-year history of Venezuela's central bank's records. Of course this growth measures in large part the rebound and recovery from the terrible damage done to the economy during the national strike in December 2002 and January 2003. Analysts are predicting much lower growth rates for 2005. Predictions notwithstanding, the GDP grew 7.9 percent in the first quarter of 2005, marking the sixth straight quarter in which the economy has expanded. From a record high of 103.2 percent in 1996, and an average of 39 percent from 1990–2003, inflation decreased to 21.7 percent in 2004, and is expected to drop to 18.2 percent in 2005.[22] The national reserves reached a record $30 billion at the end of May 2005, just under the total public debt, which is estimated at $33 billion.

While the government presents these macroeconomic indicators as evidence of the success of its policies, it also recognizes that the systematic changes it has promised to implement are slow in coming, and have yet to catch up with the revolution in the political system. For example, the government has yet to definitively incorporate the agricultural sector into the national economy as part of a broader strategy related to national security, food security, and rural stabilization.

The informal sector and unemployment remain serious national problems. As of July 2005, unemployment was hovering at around 11 percent, just slightly lower than when President Chávez took office, even though the government has added hundreds of thousands to its payroll. Despite the huge redistribution efforts, the majority of Venezuelans still live in poverty, and the income gap remains one of the worst in the region.

From a neoliberal economic perspective, Venezuela's economy is overly centralized and state dominated, with far too many controls on what should be a liberal, free market. The government should let the currency trade freely on international markets, privatize its bureaucratic state-run enterprises, remove subsidies and price controls, increase the price of gasoline, and support the establishment of the FTAA. State economic control, together with political polarization and instability, may drive away foreign investors, decrease Venezuela's credit rating, make the economy inefficient, and ultimately cost poor people jobs. Moreover, for neoliberals, the use of oil revenues to solve these problems and prop up the economy is not sustainable and merely serves to cover up the structural problems in the way Venezuela's economy is being managed.

(89) How have the changes in the economic model affected "average" people?

The stated purpose of the majority of the economic changes over the last six years is to benefit the poor majority, who still represent roughly 80 percent of the country. The increased role of the state in the economy and the redistribution of oil rents to social programs have, at least in the short term, represented significant benefits for average Venezuelans. Many of the government's social programs and missions have an impact on all Venezuelans, even those not directly involved.

Mission Mercal, as noted above, accounts for nearly half of daily food sales in the country and provides average discounts of 28 percent below market prices. Nationwide discounts on this scale inevitably impact the entire food market, slowing inflation dramatically as private distributors are forced to keep prices low to compete. This means that all Venezuelan consumers, even those who never shop in Mission Mercal depots, are benefiting from the impact that these subsidies have on the broader market.

The government maintains gasoline and diesel fuels at some of the lowest rates in the world, in spite of the recommendations of international financial institutions. Unleaded gasoline costs just 16 cents a gallon, and has hardly risen since Chávez took office, even as the price of a barrel of oil has more than quintupled. Likewise, a ticket on the metro in Caracas costs a low 16 cents. These rock-bottom prices ensure that the costs of transportation stay low, which in turn helps keep the price of basic consumer goods down.

Another economic policy that has had a direct impact on men and women working in the formal sector across Venezuela is the increases in the minimum wage. Since Chávez took office, the minimum wage has been increased on four separate occasions, so that it is outpacing inflation. In addition to the rise in basic salaries, the government has supported the distribution of "Cesta Tickets" (widely accepted food stamps) as a monthly bonus for workers in both the private and the public sector. The minimum wage is now just shy of $200 per month and medium and large employers are required to supplement this with roughly $150 in Cesta Tickets.

Some of these specific benefits do not apply to workers in the informal sector. Nonetheless, to fully appreciate the impact of the new economic model on Venezuelan consumers, one must consider the macroeconomic changes discussed above and the full spectrum of social programs that dramatically reduce basic costs for all poor families.

(90) Do the changes amount to an economic revolution?

Venezuela has undergone a series of radical structural, political, and social changes since the beginning of the Bolivarian Revolution. These changes can also be clearly seen in the country's still-developing "alternative" economic model based on including historically excluded groups and providing the most to those who have the least. Taken together, these changes amount to a revolution, but whether or not the changes in the economic sector in and of themselves amount to an economic revolution is another question.

Revolution, a time of rapid, profound change, is indeed under way. This is not a Marxist revolution by any means, however much Chávez might like to quote Karl Marx, pay tribute to Fidel Castro, or talk about twenty-first-century socialism. The democratic changes are not as rapid as many *Chavistas* would like. And yet, in the context of Venezuela's economic history, the changes set in motion in 1999 when President Chávez took office (or even if one dates the economic change process to the 1989 *Caracazo*), have been not only profound but also rapid. The model of endogenous development, worker comanagement, Mission Vuelvan Caras, the food-security doctrine, the Land Law, urban land regularization, participatory democracy, Venezuela's new international economic partnerships, its success in resisting the U.S. imposition of the FTAA, and its record-breaking economic growth have made Venezuela a world leader in alternative economic development, a model for social movements and people throughout the region and indeed the world.

The Future of the Bolivarian Revolution

(91) **What are the future prospects for President Chávez?**

According to President Chávez, the Bolivarian Revolution is an irreversible process that not even he could stop. What President Chávez is suggesting is that the Bolivarian Revolution, inevitably identified with him, will transcend him and his term in office. Contrary to what Chávez suggests, some sectors of the opposition are convinced that without him, the Bolivarian process would collapse like a house of cards. Extremists with this perspective, such as the actor Orlando Urdaneta and Félix Rodríguez (famous for his role in capturing and executing Che Guevara), have openly advocated the assassination of Chávez. Others fear that if Chávez were killed, the country would explode in a bloody civil war.

Short of killing President Chávez, the opposition seems to have few viable alternatives to get him out of office. Their recent attempts have not only failed but also ended up making him stronger. The opposition has been systematically unable to produce any political leaders to challenge Chávez, let alone a coherent political platform that is capable of winning the support of the majority of Venezuelans over the Bolivarian Revolution.

On the other hand, President Chávez's party, the MVR, has also failed to produce significant national leaders, and many of his supporters have made it clear that they hope to have him in office well after his prospective second term ends.

The next presidential election in Venezuela will be held in December 2006 because Chávez was first elected under the current constitution in 2000, and given Chávez's overwhelming popular support and the opposition's inability to produce alternative political leadership, he seems destined to be elected to another six-year term. What will happen in 2012 when President Chávez's second term is over is less clear. There may be a movement to amend the constitution to allow him to run for a third term. There may be a viable opposition candidate, or the MVR may have developed new leadership to replace him. But with or without President Chávez, the millions of people who are direct beneficiaries of the peaceful Bolivarian Revolution will likely struggle to defend their newfound political power and social inclusion.

(92) **Will there be another coup attempt?**

Analysts from both ends of the political spectrum in Venezuela agree that another coup attempt is unlikely. The opposition failed not only in the April 2002 coup, but also in the series of attempts to oust President Chávez thereafter, including the December 2002 national strike and the August 2004 recall referendum. This series of failures led to the further disintegration of the opposition domestically, and to their being discredited internationally. It is unlikely that they will be able to organize internally or receive the external support necessary for a coup attempt.

More specifically, the private media has been discredited in the eyes of millions of Venezuelans, and the state now has a rapidly developing communications machine of its own to counterbalance the opposition media. President Chávez's public approval ratings have steadily risen since April 2002, depriving the opposition of any meaningful base of support. Finally, the strong alliance between the civilian and the military sectors supporting President Chávez creates a virtually impregnable defense for his government.

The strengthening of the government in all of these areas has led many commentators to speculate that rather than mount another coup attempt, the extremists in the opposition will attempt to assassinate Chávez. On countless occasions, Chávez himself has accused the opposition and even the U.S. government of having plans to assassinate him, though he has yet to produce any intelligence to support that claim.

(93) Will Venezuela's democracy become a dictatorship?

It is unlikely that Venezuela's democracy will become a dictatorship, primarily because of the government's commitment to deepening democratic institutions and practices. The government's track record, beginning with a broadly inclusive, participatory, democratic constitutional assembly, is not dictatorial. The government has even established a new Ministry of Participation, to focus exclusively on expanding popular participation in the political process.

The opposition's criticisms of Chávez's consolidation of power and the calls for Chávez to stay in office "until 2021" have led many to speculate that he does not intend to step down after his prospective second term is up. If President Chávez did decide to run for president again in 2012, it would only be possible through an amendment to the constitution. Though unlikely, this is a possibility, depending on the political developments over the next six years. It is worth pointing out that President Uribe of Colombia has already successfully enlisted the support of the U.S. government and a wide range of his domestic supporters for precisely that kind of amendment to the Colombian constitution so that he will be able to run for reelection in 2006.

In any case, the issue of a Chávez "dictatorship" in Venezuela has largely ceased to be a topic of interest even among the opposition and the private media. Since the 2004 recall referendum the accusations of dictatorship have largely disappeared—the democratic track record of the government speaks for itself.

(94) What changes can be expected in terms of freedom of speech?

Since the Social Responsibility in Radio and Television Law was approved, the news cycle has moved on to other issues, and the criticisms of the law have faded from the front pages of opposition newspapers. The media continue their attacks against the government, but the issue of freedom of speech is no longer a lead issue.

Independent Venezuelan artists and musicians are the ones celebrating the new media law: their skills and talent are suddenly in high demand. Venezuela has a rich musical and artistic tradition to tap into, but for years local artists could not compete with Britney Spears or the Backstreet Boys for airtime on corporate-controlled radio. For example, under the new law there has been a resurgence of the traditional *llanero* music from the plains states of Venezuela.

The general political situation in Venezuela makes it hard to imagine the kind of hostility that existed between the government and the corporate media in 2002. The government is determined to continue promoting alternatives to private media outlets. Venezuela is thus likely to experience a proliferation of a diverse group of media outlets—from independent producers and artists to community-based radio stations and state-sponsored international networks like Telesur. This process is already under way, and represents not only a guarantee that freedom of speech cannot be hijacked by either the government or corporate monopolies but also a shift toward a new kind of freedom of speech, where the people themselves play a leading role in the formation of public opinion. The fate of this kind of participatory government depends, to a large extent, on the people's ability to access and influence national and international media.

While the extensive role of the state in the media remains problematic, it exists in the context of a monopolistic private media that had acquired an inordinate amount of political power. International NGOs and human rights groups, together with the Venezuelan private media, have proven themselves vigilant watchdogs of the Venezuelan government on freedom of speech issues, and there is no sign of that changing in the near future. Venezuela's vision for popular inclusion and diversification of media outlets seems to be spreading beyond its borders. On May 24, 2005, Telesur ran its first trial programming, heralding the beginning of the first non-corporate-controlled international news source for, by, and about Latin Americans.

(95) Will corruption continue unabated?

Definitely.

Corruption is, to a greater or lesser extent, a problem throughout the world. It is endemic in almost every government in Latin America. Over the forty years of representative democracy, Venezuelan government developed a culture of corruption. Most Venezuelans came to accept that corruption pervaded virtually every level of their government and society. Successfully fighting corruption in Venezuela requires a change in culture and expectations across the country, and that inevitably takes time.

There have been major improvements in fighting government corruption since the beginning of the Bolivarian Revolution. On the other hand, there have been emblematic cases of corruption, such as when the vice minister of finance went on a $10,000 Christmas shopping spree in Miami, or when a government official used funds destined for the mayor of Guayana City to build a private ostrich farm. Even President Chávez admits that his government has been unable to efficiently prosecute known cases of corruption.

The government should increase its efforts to prosecute corruption within its own ranks. The independence and efficacy of the judicial system and the prosecutorial process need to be dramatically improved. No matter how well thought out the anticorruption policies or institutional reforms, it is hard to imagine a significant reduction in corruption until the political culture and national mentality begin to catch up with the ideals of the revolution.

(96) What are the prospects for the development of Venezuela's political economy?

Venezuela's nascent successes in economic policy are almost entirely dependent on the space created by its political and oil policies. The Bolivarian government is still in the process of consolidating its political model and bringing about a change of political culture both within the government and within society as a whole. This internal process also depends on deepening and extending Latin American and Caribbean integration as well as alliances and treaties with countries as far away as China and Iran.

For the foreseeable future, the oil industry will continue to play a key role in Venezuela's economic development. International oil markets continue to be the single most influential factor in determining the prospects for Venezuela's political economy. Oil rents hold the key to a diversified, endogenously developed economy, but also could continue to drown out other sectors of Venezuela's economy in mono-export dependency. At this point, if the international oil markets collapsed, Venezuela's economy would go with them. The Chávez government is investing heavily in the future through its education and health-care programs, in addition to supporting endogenous development initiatives, but those investments will take years to pay off.

The future of Venezuela's economy will depend in large part on the government's domestic strength and its ability to implement strong foreign and oil policy. Luckily for the government, it has never been stronger domestically, and oil prices seem to be holding fast at record highs. As of now, Venezuela's economy continues to outperform analysts' predictions.

(97) What are the prospects for Venezuela's oil industry?

If the government is able to accomplish its stated goals, Venezuela could develop into a diversified economy in which petroleum would cease to be the sole engine driving it. The government's heavy investment in social programs has drained the oil sector of needed investments. Perhaps these investments in education, in job training, and in health care will allow Venezuela to develop other sectors of its economy even as the oil sector becomes less profitable due to some combination of underinvestment and changes in the global energy markets. On the other hand, if the investments fail to substantially develop new areas of the economy, Venezuela could be left not only without the current backbone of its national economy, but also with nothing to replace it.

Venezuela is still making both political and capital investments in its petroleum sector. If Venezuela is able to solidify Petroamérica, then it may be able to allocate even more oil rents for developing other sectors of the economy. If the government can get international oil companies to agree to the oil tax law being enforced retroactively, then it will substantially increase state revenue from oil production, even if overall production decreases. If Venezuela is able to consolidate its nascent attempts at diversifying its market beyond U.S. buyers, it may be able to use its petroleum sales to develop a wide range of international alliances, though this may further jeopardize bilateral relations with the U.S. government.

Whatever else happens, in the short and medium term, petroleum will definitely continue to be the backbone of the economy and the key to Venezuela's foreign policy. How to best invest the country's oil wealth remains an open question, and one that will likely be controversial for years to come.

(98) What are the prospects for the development of the missions?

There are two leading theories about what will happen to the missions. One suggests that they will be assimilated into traditional state institutions, such as the ministries. For example, Mission Vuelvan Caras may become part of the Ministry of Popular Economy, and so on. The second theory argues that the missions will themselves absorb part of the state. For example, the success of Mission Barrio Adentro is unlikely to be sustainable if it becomes part of the central government bureaucracy, especially given the limited coverage and inefficiency in the Ministry of Health. It is perhaps more likely that Barrio Adentro will absorb or replace the Ministry of Health.

A third possibility, perhaps the most likely, is some combination of the above. In this case the missions and the ministries would develop an integrated dual capacity, with the balance between them depending on the particular case. The government has suggested that some missions, such as the adult literacy–oriented Mission Robinson, will have a limited tenure. Other missions, such as Mission Habitat, could easily be continued indefinitely to meet the constantly burgeoning demand for affordable housing, or even be expanded to support small businesses. In any case, what has happened thus far amounts to the creation of a parallel bureaucracy, and it is not likely to be sustainable in the long term to maintain two state social systems at once.

(99) Will Venezuela cut off relations with Colombia and the United States?

It is highly doubtful that Venezuela will cut off its bilateral relations with either Colombia or the United States because of its mutual dependence with both of these countries. Despite the political tensions that exist between

Colombia and Venezuela, both governments have been able to find speedy diplomatic solutions to their problems. They continue to be each other's second-largest trading partners and to cooperate on a range of bilateral projects. These two countries have historical, geographical, and cultural ties, and they each have substantial populations of each other's nationals living in their territory.

In the case of the United States, despite the hostile rhetoric from both sides, trade has continued unabated, and the United States is still Venezuela's largest trading partner. Given the U.S. dependency on Venezuela for roughly 12 percent of its daily oil imports, it is hard to imagine a scenario where the United States would willingly cut off economic relations. In light of repeated U.S. government acknowledgements, however qualified, that Venezuela is a democracy, and the United States' long-term military commitments in Iraq, Afghanistan, and other areas of the world, it is hard to fathom a U.S. military intervention. Some Venezuelans on both sides of the political spectrum continue to speculate about the possibility. It is probable, however, that the United States will continue its political-electoral intervention in Venezuela in the name of "supporting democracy," as indicated by President Bush's May 31, 2005, meeting with María Corina Machado, one of the leaders of Venezuela's opposition "civil society." Funding supporting political-opposition groups like Machado's Súmate is likely to peak as the 2006 election approaches. Similarly, funding for the Colombian military is likely to continue well beyond the elections.

U.S. government spokespeople and policy makers have repeatedly stated their intention to continue supporting opposition political groups. This fact, together with President Chávez's hard-line rhetoric, makes it unlikely that diplomatic relations between Venezuela and the United States will improve as long as President Chávez is in office.

In the spring of 2005, President Chávez began speaking regularly about supposed U.S.-government-supported plans to assassinate him and/or to invade Venezuela. He emphasized that if either were to happen, Venezuela would be prepared to use asymmetrical warfare to defend its sovereignty and that the United States would never receive another drop of Venezuelan oil. Clearly this would be an extreme situation, which makes predictions unreliable at best. Critics have suggested that Chávez uses these assertions to distract Venezuelans from domestic problems and to rally his supporters.

Regardless of the contingency plans being debated in Washington and Caracas, their mutual dependence, and Venezuela's continually expanding international alliances, will make it difficult for Washington to isolate Venezuela. Or at least that is what President Chávez is banking on.

(100) What are the future prospects for the Bolivarian Revolution?

Although the national and international campaign against the Bolivarian Revolution continues, with each day that passes it seems there are fewer internal obstacles and a deeper level of "revolutionary consciousness" from Chávez's popular support base. Chávez's approval ratings have never been higher, and his consolidation of government power is starting to yield results.

It is also true that Chávez's goals for the peaceful, democratic revolution cannot possibly be accomplished in the short term. Chávez himself has put out the date of 2021 as the minimum amount of time needed, and that may not be nearly enough time to accomplish some of the ambitious goals he has set for the revolution. More than simply consolidating control of the government and defeating repeated internal and external opposition attempts to undermine it, the Bolivarian Revolution will have to continue developing sound policy alternatives to those being implemented the world over, and to incorporate at least some sectors of groups such as the middle class that currently lean toward the opposition. Perhaps most significantly, it will need new leadership to replace President Chávez after his second term in office.

Internally, the Venezuelan process is already on the verge of accomplishing some of its immediate goals, such as universal health care and zero illiteracy. Through concrete achievements like these, the Bolivarian Revolution has provided the world with an alternative vision to the Washington-dominated neoliberal economic and neoconservative political policies. The broad commitment to endogenous development through an industrialized, diversified economy based on worker-comanaged companies and cooperatives may allow Venezuela to break out of the dependence on transnational capital that traps so many countries. Its inclusive economic model may make the high social costs of competing for direct foreign investments with countries like China, Haiti, and Malaysia a thing of the past. Indeed, rather than competing with other poor countries, Venezuela has aggressively pursued new alliances and bilateral treaties as a way to both cooperate with the global south and to free itself from a historic dependence on the United States. The consolidation, however contested, of the European Union as a political-economic group has given new life to Simón Bolívar's dream of Latin American unity.

Internationally, President Chávez and the Bolivarian Revolution have begun to win a following. Millions have found in Chávez what their own politicians lack: hope, vision, charisma, steadfast commitment to the poor and, perhaps most significant, the courage to stand up for his people, even in the face of a hostile U.S. government. If Chávez has his way, the world will no longer be defined by a sole superpower, but will become multipolar. The Left in Latin America has made significant gains in electoral contests since Chávez was first elected. To what extent these gains can be directly attributed to Chávez is an open question, but it is clear that he and the Bolivarian Revolution have changed the stakes and the terms for would-be leaders throughout the region. The 2006 Latin American election cycle, which includes nine separate countries, may be decisive in determining the future of the relationship between the United States and the entire region. Venezuela's next presidential election, in December 2006, will be the key to the future of the Bolivarian Revolution.

NOTES

1. Anderson, Jon Lee. "Looking for *El Libertador*," *The New Yorker*, September 10, 2001.
2. Some commentators continue to deny the obvious. For example, in late 2004 Damarys Canache wrote: "Largely because of [the support of the poor], the Chávez presidency enjoyed a prolonged honeymoon period, but the pragmatism of the urban poor suggests that this honeymoon will not last indefinitely. Chávez's failure to transform symbolic action into substantive results has created mounting frustration among a wide spectrum of Venezuelan society, including a significant portion of the urban poor." These assertions become almost laughable in light of the above-cited poll data, not to mention the opinions that the residents of Caracas's barrios will readily offer anyone who takes the time to listen. Quoted from Damarys Canache's essay "Urban Poor and Political Order" in *The Unraveling of Representative Democracy in Venezuela* edited by Jennifer McCoy and David Myers. Baltimore: Johns Hopkins Press, 2004, 47–48.
3. From 1994 to 1999 Rafael Caldera, one of the founders of the COPEI party, was president, though in the 1993 election he ran as an independent without the official support of his party.
4. Although these are the official numbers according to the CNE, many sources, also citing CNE, attribute just 56 percent of the vote in this election to Chávez and nearly 40 percent to his closest competitor.
5. Kelly, Janet, and Romero, Carlos A. *The United States and Venezuela: Rethinking a Relationship*. New York: Routledge, 2002, 90.
6. López Maya, Margarita, "Hugo Chávez Frías: His Movement and His

Presidency," in *Venezuelan Politics in the Chávez Era: Class, Polarization, and Conflict*, edited by Steve Ellner and Daniel Hellinger. Boulder: Lynne Rienner Publishers, 2003, 89.

7. Viciano Pastor, Roberto and Martínez Dalmau, Rubén. *Cambio político y proceso constituyente en Venezuela*, 1998–2000.

8. Molina, José, E. "The Unraveling of Venezuela's Party System: From Party Rule to Personalistic Politics and Deinstitutionalization," in *The Unraveling of Representative Democracy in Venezuela*.

9. Going further, some critics, such as Rafael de la Cruz, argue that the Chávez government "has not promulgated a single regulation that would advance the decentralization process." Cruz, Rafael de la, "Decentralization: Key to Understanding a Changing Nation," in *The Unraveling of Representative Democracy in Venezuela*.

10. *Aló Presidente*, no. 193; Santa Inés, Barinas, June 13, 2004.

11. Reuters, "Venezuela, Brazil world leaders in gun deaths—UN," *New York Times*, May 5, 2005.

12. Article 82: "Every person has the right to adequate, safe and comfortable, hygienic housing, with appropriate essential basic services, including a habitat such as to humanize family, neighborhood, and community relations. The Progressive meeting of this requirement is the shared responsibility of citizens and the State in all areas.

   The State shall give priority to families, and shall guarantee them, especially those with meager resources, the possibility of access to social policies and credit for the construction, purchase or enlargement of dwellings."

13. This presidential right is currently established in article 192 of the Organic Law of Telecommunications. The law has long been on the books in Venezuela, but became a political issue under President Chávez because he is the first president to regularly invoke this right, much to the chagrin of the private media and many a baseball fan and soap opera aficionado whose programs are interrupted all too often.

14. Hernandez Montoya, Roberto, "El Terrorismo considerado como una de las bellas artes," *Question*, March 2003, 9.

15. Energy Information Administration, Department of Energy Oil Briefing www.eia.doe.gov/oiaf/archive/ieo00/oil.html

16. Mommer, Bernard. "Subversive Oil," in *Venezuelan Politics in the Chávez Era*.

17. Chávez, Hugo, and Harnecker, Marta. *Understanding the Venezuelan Revolution: Hugo Chávez Talks to Marta Harnecker*, translated by Chesa Boudin. Monthly Review Press, 2005.

18. From an unpublished working paper titled "Walking on Two Legs," made available to authors.

19. *Aló Presidente*, no. 206; From the Bramon Coffee Cooperative, Junin municipality, Táchira State, June 10, 2004.

20. UNICEF Venezuela Country Info http://www.unicef.org/infobycountry/ venezuela_statistics.html

21. CIA World Factbook Venezuela.

22. IMF World Economic Outlook, April 2005, cited in *Latin Business Chronicle*, available at http://www.latinbusinesschronicle.com/statistics/ inflation/overview.htm.

SUGGESTIONS FOR FURTHER READING

Books and Articles

Aguirre, Jesús María, Cañizales, Andrés and Pellegrino, Francisco. *Los medios de comunicación en Venezuela*. Curso de Formación Sociopolítica # 26. Fundación Centro Gumilla, Caracas, 1999.

Bilbao, Luis. "Chávez y la revolución bolivariana (conversaciones con Luis Bilbao)." *Le Monde Diplomatique*, 3rd edition, Caracas, 2002.

Bolívar, Simón. *Obras Completas, t. III: Discurso de Angostura*. Editorial Lec, La Havana, 1950.

Boue, Juan Carlos. *La internacionalización de Pdvsa: una costosa ilusión*. Fondo Editorial Darío Ramírez, Ministerio de Energía y Minas, Caracas, 2004.

Brito García, Luis. "Investigación de unos medios por encima de toda sospecha." *Question*. Caracas, 2003.

Cañizales, Andrés and Correa, Carlos. *Informe 2002: Venezuela, situación del derecho a la libertad de expresión e información*. Konrad Adenauer Stiftung—Espacio Público, Caracas, 2003.

Chávez, Hugo. *2004: Año de logros*. Ministerio de Comunicación e Información, Caracas, 2005.

Coronil, Fernando. *The Magical State: Nature, Money, and Modernity in Venezuela*. University of Chicago Press, 1997.

Correa, Juan. *Cronología de un golpe de Estado*. Imprenta Nacional. Caracas, 2002.

Dietrich, Heinz. *La Operación Rescate de la Dignidad Nacional*. La Burbuja Editorial, Caracas, 2002.

Elizalde, Rosa Miriam and Báez, Luis. *Chávez Nuestro.* Casa Editorial Abril, La Havana, 2004.

Ellner, Steve, and Daniel Hellinger, eds. *Venezuelan Politics in the Chávez Era: Class, Polarization, and Conflict.* Lynne Rienner Publishers, 2003.

Golinger, Eva. *The Chávez Code: Cracking U.S. Intervention in Venezuela.* Editorial Jose Marti, 2005.

Gott, Richard. *Hugo Chávez: The Bolivarian Revolution in Venezuela.* Verso, 2005.

González, Gabriel. *El golpe de Estado Constitucional.* La Burbuja Editorial, Caracas, 2005.

Karl, Terry Lynn. *The Paradox of Plenty: Oil Booms and Petro-States (Studies in International Political Economy, No. 26).* University of California Press, 1997.

Kelly, Janet, and Romero, Carlos A. *United States and Venezuela: Rethinking a Relationship.* Routledge, 2001.

McCoy, Jennifer, and Myers, David, eds. *The Unraveling of Representative Democracy in Venezuela.* Johns Hopkins Press, 2004.

Ortiz, Eduardo F. *Análisis socioeconómico de Venezuela.* Curso de formación sociopolítica # 8. Fundación Centro Gumilla, Publicaciones de la Universidad Católica Andrés Bello, Caracas, 2004.

Quiroz, Rafael. *El Convenio petrolero con Cuba.* La Burbuja Editorial, Caracas, 2002.

Viciano Pastor, Roberto and Martínez Dalmau, Rubén. *Cambio político y proceso constituyente en Venezuela (1998–2000).* Vadell Hermanos Editores, Valencia, 2001.

Wilpert, Gregory. *The Rise and Fall of Hugo Chávez: Revolution and Counter-Revolution in Venezuela.* Zed Books, 2005.

Legal Documents

Constitution of the Bolivarian Republic of Venezuela, 1999.

Ley Orgánica de Hidrocarburos, 2001.

Ley de Pesca y Acuicultura, 2001.

Ley de Responsabilidad Social en Radio y Televisión, 2004.

Ley de Tierras y Desarrollo Agrario, 2001.

Ley de Creacion, Estimulo, Promocion y Desarrollo del Sistema Microfinanciero, 2001.

Web Pages

www.aporrea.org, a Web site dedicated to supporting the Bolivarian Revolution through news, information, and promoting popular participation

www.bcv.gov.ve, the Web site for the Central Bank of Venezuela

www.el-nacional.com, the Web site for one of Venezuela's major daily news papers representing the opposition,

www.eluniversal.com, the Web site for another one of Venezuela's major daily newspapers representing the opposition

www.ine.gov.ve, the Web site for Venezuela's National Institute for Statistics, includes a wide range of demographic and social indicator statistics

www.mci.gov.ve, the Web site for the Ministry of Communication and Information, essentially the spokesperson for the government

www.rebelion.org, an alternative, noncommercial, left-wing news source focusing on Venezuela

www.rnv.gov.ve, Venezuelan National Radio, a government news source

www.ultimasnoticias.com.ve, Venezuela's largest circulating daily newspaper, more moderate than *El Universal* or *El Nacional*

www.vcrisis.com, staunchly anti-Chávez Venezuela news and analysis blog

www.venezuelanalysis.com, in depth English language Venezuela news and analysis sympathetic to the objectives of the Revolution

www.venezuelafoia.info, the Web site with the files detailing the role of the US government in the April 2002 coup

Documentary Films

The Revolution Will Not Be Televised, Directed by Kim Bartley and Donnacha O Briain, Produced by the Irish Film Board

Llaguno Bridge: Keys to a Massacre, Directed by Angel Palacios, Produced by Panafilms, 2004

Venezuela Bolivariana: Pueblo y Lucha de la IV Guerra Mundial, Directed by Marcelo Andrade Arreaza, Produced by Calle Y Media Colectivo, 2004

Acknowledgments

This group effort included input and support from more than just the three coauthors. We have Sam Kass to thank for his suggestions, which began when we were finishing the first draft. At the last minute, Bill Ayers, Kathy Boudin, Bernardine Dohrn, Jonah Gindin, Elizabeth Joynes, Michael Lebowitz, and Sarah Stillman all took the time to read drafts or partial drafts and give us comments. A special thanks to Michelle Martin and John Oakes at Avalon for their support for the book from the beginning. John's feedback and willingness to discuss the direction of the book was a great help throughout. Thanks also to Alex, Marta, Max, Carmen, and Luis in Venezuela. Finally, each of us has our families to thank for their support throughout the process.

Author Bios

Chesa Boudin is a summa cum laude graduate of Yale University with a degree in history. While at Yale he studied at the University of Chile for a year. His work has been published in *The Nation*, the *Chicago Tribune*, and *Salon.com*, and his first book *Letters From Young Activists*, was published in 2005 by Nation Books. He has a master's degree in forced migration and is currently working on a second master's degree in public policy in Latin America at Oxford University on a Rhodes Scholarship.

Gabriel González is a graduate of the Central University of Venezuela with a degree in literature. His books previously published in Venezuela and Ecuador include: *Lo que pasa en Venezuela o el golpe que vendrá, Manual del dirigente, La fotografía de El Cojo ilustrado: o de cómo se construyó un país virtual en el imaginario de una élite de lectores,* and *Mirada y Transparencia de los adioses.* He currently works as an analyst for President Chávez's team of advisors.

Wilmer Rumbos is a graduate of the Central University of Venezuela with a degree in journalism and social communication. He has worked as a freelance journalist and photographer and also as a full-time reporter for the weekly Venezuelan political magazine *Tribuna popular.* From 2001–2003 he hosted a popular political radio program called *Contacto Laboral.* He currently lectures on photography at the Central University of Venezuela and has a weekly column published in Venezuela's widest-circulating daily newspaper *Últimas Noticias.*